Using the

CALIFORNIA STYLE MANUAL

and

THE BLUEBOOK:

A Practitioner's Guide

By Susan Heinrich-Wells

Adjunct Faculty Member
California Western School of Law

D0973425

WEST GROUP

San Francisco
2000

© 2000 by West Group
All rights reserved.

ISBN 0-314-24856-0

Page composition by ImageInk, San Francisco

West Group
50 California Street
San Francisco, CA 94111

For customer assistance, please call 1-800-328-4880.

About the Author

Susan Heinrich-Wells is a graduate of Suffolk University School of Law, Boston, Massachusetts. She is licensed to practice before all state and federal courts in California and in the federal courts in Hawaii. From 1990 to 1995, she was associated with a San Diego firm specializing in admiralty law and the defense of policyholders for insurers at Lloyd's of London, including vessel owners, shipyards, and related waterfront industries. She formed her own firm in 1995 and expanded her practice to include litigation of leasing disputes for commercial landlords. Currently she is general counsel for a property asset and management company in San Diego and teaches insurance law at California Western School of Law, where she is an adjunct faculty member.

TABLE OF CONTENTS

Tables

INTRODUCTION

The idea for this book has its roots in the frustration of an East Coast–educated lawyer who was bred on *The Bluebook: A Uniform System of Citation*, and then transplanted to California where the *California Style Manual* is also used. As the promulgator and recipient of a multitude of legal memoranda and briefs, it has been my observation that there is confusion among California practitioners regarding citation format and which style manual to use in which court. This confusion exists regardless of whether practitioners were educated in California law schools or elsewhere. This guide is intended to quell the confusion and foster precision and uniformity in legal memoranda and briefs filed in California courts.

Why Confusion Reigns in California Courts

Part of the confusion and inconsistency among practitioners is attributable to the inaccessibility of the *California Style Manual*. Prior to West Group publishing the fourth edition of the *California Style Manual* in 2000, the Publication Section of the Department of General Services (DGS) published the manual. Copies were not generally available on bookstore shelves. To obtain a *California Style Manual*, one had to write (no phone calls, please) to the DGS and request a copy. DGS would write back requesting payment in advance. The process took several weeks. In short, the *California Style Manual* was hard to get. No doubt this was one reason why California law schools taught from the *Bluebook* rather than the *California Style Manual*. In any event, it is now more accessible and, therefore, likely to be used with greater frequency by practitioners.

Another reason that neither the *California Style Manual* nor the *Bluebook* is used consistently or accurately is because they are lengthy and necessarily complex. When it comes to filing a brief or memorandum, a practitioner's foremost concern is meeting the deadline. Style takes a backseat to substance. It takes time to look up rules of citation and many lawyers do not have the time or get frustrated and give up, thinking it will not really make a difference. We cite cases as they are cited in practice guides, unofficial reporters, and computer databases. And we are therefore getting further and further away from the uniform language we are supposed to speak as attorneys licensed to practice law in the same state.

Additionally, another reason for confusion is that local court rules previously expressed a preference for one style manual over the other. While Rule 313(e) of the California Rules of Court allows use of either the *Bluebook* or the *California Style Manual* in state courts, up until recently, individual trial courts promulgated local rules indicating a preference. For example, Rule 4.1(f) of the San Diego County Superior Court Rules provided that "Citations of cases shall be by reference to the official reporter and shall indicate the volume number, the first page of the case, and the specific page or pages on which the pertinent matters appear in the official reports, and the year of the decision." This format (requiring a point page and the year placed at the end of the citation) is consistent with the *Bluebook*, not the *California Style Manual*. In theory, if you used the *California Style Manual* format in San Diego Superior Court, the clerk had the power to reject your filing for failure to comply with local rules. Hence a practitioner could not rely solely on either the *California Style Manual* or the *Bluebook* as prescribed by the California Rules of Court. It was necessary to confer with the local rules of each trial court.

This dilemma ended on July 1, 1997, when the Judicial Council enacted Rule 302 of the California Rules of Court. Rule 302 renders any local rule concerning form or format of papers, motions, demurrers, discovery, or pleadings null and void. Form or format is now the exclusive domain of the Judicial Council. Effective July 1, 2000, Rule 981.1 supersedes Rule 302, but the intent to preempt local rules is the same. The only *statewide* rule that applies is Rule 313(e), which allows for the use of *either* style manual. Rule 302 (or Rule 981.1 in July 2000) renders it a little bit easier for busy practitioners to file more professional work product without the burden of untangling a web of rules.

When to Use the *California Style Manual* versus the *Bluebook*

The general rule is that one should use the *California Style Manual* in all state courts because the judges do. While Rule 313(e) allows for use of either the *California Style Manual* or the *Bluebook* in state courts, use of the *California Style Manual* is preferred. This is indicated by the title to Rule 313(e), which reads: "[Use of the California Style Manual]." It does not read "[Use of the California Style Manual or the Uniform System of Citation]." Just as a dictionary indicates a preferred use by the order in which a word appears, so does Rule 313(e). The *California Style Manual* is mentioned before the *Bluebook*, indicating its use is preferred.

That aside, the most compelling reason for a state court practitioner to choose the *California Style Manual* is that state court judges, research attorneys, and law clerks use it. Why they use it is clear when the origins of the *California Style Manual* are known.

The California Supreme Court has a constitutional and statutory obligation to oversee the publication of its official decisions and those of the courts of appeal. It delegates this responsibility to its Reporter of Decisions. The first Reporter of Decisions was the renowned Bernard E. Witkin, who created the *California Style Manual* in 1942 as a means of fulfilling this responsibility. It was designed as a guide for legal publishers, presumably to bridge gaps in the *Bluebook* regarding the citation of legal materials unique to California. Its goal was "to state the chief rules and practices which govern the preparation, form and publication of opinions of the appellate courts of California."[1] Since the *California Style Manual*, which is copyrighted by the California Supreme Court, is utilized by California's highest court of review and courts of appeal, it is also relied on by trial courts.

Logically enough, if a practitioner's brief is prepared using the *California Style Manual*, it will resemble an official decision. Psychologically, this is bound to affect the way one's brief is viewed and read. If it looks ready to print, it is more palatable to the research attorneys reading it; and, of course, it is easier for them to do their job. The more we speak the same language as the judges and their staff, the easier we are able to communicate and be understood and the more readily our positions can be adopted.

The rule for use of the *Bluebook* is straightforward: use it in federal courts unless it is silent on citing a particular authority, then use the *California Style Manual*. The *Bluebook*, now in its sixteenth edition, is compiled by the editors of the Columbia Law Review, the Harvard Law Review, the University of Pennsylvania Law Review, and the Yale Law Review. It is designed for a national audience and includes abbreviations and citations covering all 50 states and the District of Columbia and other federal jurisdictions. In practice, it is the style manual preferred by federal courts.

Sometimes, however, the *Bluebook* does not address a specific reference unique to California, such as California jury instructions in civil cases (BAJI). The *California Style Manual* does, however, and should be consulted whenever the *Bluebook* is silent on a subject.

---

1 Witkin, Bernard E., preface to the first edition, reprinted in *California Style Manual: A Handbook of Legal Style for California Courts and Lawyers*, 3d ed. (San Francisco: Supreme Court of California, 1986).

How to Use This Guide

This handy reference guide contains a compilation of the *California Style Manual* and *Bluebook* rules used most frequently by practitioners, presented side by side, and accessible by a single index. Hence, a busy practitioner rushing to meet a filing deadline in the United States District Court for the Central District of California and in Orange County Superior Court need only consult this guide to determine how to correctly cite California case law in the federal court (using *Bluebook* format) and the state court (using *California Style Manual* format). In addition to specific examples, this guide also highlights the dissimilarities between the two style manuals in a memorable fashion so that the process of submitting a polished work product becomes more automatic and less laborious. This guide is not intended to replace either the *California Style Manual* or the *Bluebook*, but should be considered an abridged compilation of both, specifically tailored to meet the day-to-day needs of practitioners. It is also ideal for law students who are learning their way around both manuals.

Our basic need to access information quickly and easily is why the *California Style Manual* and the *Bluebook* were created: to ensure uniformity and accessibility to the official reports of the courts, legislative materials, legal texts and publications. As described by one author, "Admittedly, the rules of legal citation may be overly complex. Even so, they serve important purposes by ensuring that essential information is conveyed in a concise manner, and minimizing wasted time in trying to decipher the authority being cited."[2]

Citations are our language, our access code to galaxies of legal precedent. We must know this language to preserve the integrity of the system, to show deference to the judges and research attorneys who read our work product, and to give rise to a sense of reliability and professionalism in our written word. This is no small thing, and with this guide, it need not be too time-consuming or frustrating.

San Diego   Susan Heinrich-Wells
February 2000

---

2 Eisenberg et al., Cal. Practice Guide: Civil Appeals and Writs (The Rutter Group 1999) ¶ 9:43, p. 9-12 (rev. #1, 1999).

—Notes—

—Notes—

CALIFORNIA OPINIONS AND BASIC STYLE ELEMENTS

§ 1:1   Citations to official case reporter

General rule: In the California Style Manual,[1] the title of the case is in italics, followed by the year of decision in parentheses, the volume number of the official reporter, an abbreviation for the official reporter, and the page number followed by a period. If the cited authority does not form an integral part of the sentence (i.e., the meaning of the sentence is not altered when the citation is deleted), it is enclosed in parentheses regardless of where it appears in the text.

---

1 Jessen, Edward W., *California Style Manual: A Handbook of Legal Style for California Courts and Lawyers*, 4th ed. (San Francisco: Supreme Court of California, 2000).

In The Bluebook: A Uniform System of Citation (hereafter the Bluebook),[2] the title of the case is either underscored or italicized, followed by a comma, the volume number of the official reporter, an abbreviation for the official reporter, the page number and the year of the decision enclosed in parentheses and followed by a period.

California Style Manual:

(*Betts v. Allstate Insurance Company* (1984) 154 Cal.App.3d 688.)

An insurer's refusal to accept a settlement offer within policy limits may constitute bad faith. (*Betts v. Allstate Insurance Company* (1984) 154 Cal.App.3d 688.)

Insurers may be held liable for bad faith for failing to settle a case within policy limits (*Betts v. Allstate Insurance Company* (1984) 154 Cal.App.3d 688), or for failing to promptly investigate the claim (*Egan v. Mutual of Omaha Insurance Co.* (1979) 24 Cal.3d 809.).

In *Betts v. Allstate Insurance Company* (1984) 154 Cal.App.3d 688, the court addressed the issue of whether an insurer's refusal to accept a settlement offer within policy limits constituted bad faith.

Bluebook:

Betts v. Allstate Insurance Company, 154 Cal._App._3d 688 (1984).[3]

An insurer's refusal to accept a settlement offer within policy limits may constitute bad faith. *Betts v. Allstate Insurance Company*, 154 Cal._App._3d 688 (1984).

Insurers may be held liable for bad faith for failing to settle a case within policy limits, *Betts v. Allstate Insurance Company*, 154 Cal.App.3d 688 (1984), or for failing to promptly investigate the claim, *Egan v. Mutual of Omaha Insurance Co.*, 24 Cal._3d 809 (1979).

In *Betts v. Allstate Insurance Company*, 154 Cal._App._3d 688 (1984), the court addressed the issue of whether an insurer's refusal to accept a settlement offer within policy limits constituted bad faith.

Case names: Case names (including the "v." for versus) are italicized in both manuals. The Bluebook also allows the case name to be underscored instead of italicized as illustrated in the second Bluebook example above.

---

2 The Bluebook: A Uniform System of Citation, 16th ed. (Cambridge: The Harvard Law Review Association, 1996).

3 Underscoring is used for illustrative purposes only to emphasize the spacing that distinguishes Bluebook abbreviations from those used by the California Style Manual.

Year: Apparently, the California Style Manual considers the year in which a case was decided second only in importance to its name. The year follows the case name without a comma. The Bluebook, on the other hand, places the year in parentheses at the end of the citation.

Parentheses: The California Style Manual ordinarily places citations within parentheses, regardless of where the citation appears in the sentence. (See the first through third examples above.) However, if the citation is an integral part of the sentence (such that deleting it would change the meaning of the sentence), no parentheses are used. (See the fourth example above.)

The Bluebook, on the other hand, uses commas instead of parentheses to separate the citation from the rest of the sentence. (See the third and fourth examples above.) Ordinarily, only the year of decision is enclosed in parentheses.

Commas: Only the Bluebook uses a comma between the case name and the volume number of the reporter.

Cross-references: Cal. Style Manual § 1:1[B], [D], and [E]. Bluebook, Practitioners' Notes, P.1(a), p. 11; see also Rule 1.6, pp. 28–30.

Table 1
Citations to Official Case Reporter

California Style Manual	Bluebook
(*Mercy Hospital and Medical Center v. Farmers Insurance Group of Companies* (1997) 15 Cal.4th 213.)	*Mercy Hospital and Medical Center v. Farmers Insurance Group of Companies,* 15 Cal._4th 213 (1997).[a]
	or
	<u>Mercy Hospital and Medical Center v. Farmers Insurance Group of Companies,</u> 15 Cal._4th 213 (1997).
(*Betts v. Allstate Insurance Company* (1984) 154 Cal.App.3d 688.)	*Betts v. Allstate Insurance Company,* 154 Cal._App._3d 688 (1984).
(*Blue v. Los Angeles Unified School District* (1994) 26 Cal.App.4th Supp. 12.)	*Blue v. Los Angeles Unified School District,* 26 Cal._App._4th_Supp. 12 (1994).
(*People v. Bloyd* (1987) 143 Cal.3d 333.)	*People v. Bloyd,* 143 Cal._3d 333 (1987).

Table 1—*Continued*

California Style Manual	Bluebook
(*In re Trombley* (1948) 31 Cal.2d 801.)	*In re Trombley*, 31 Cal._2d 801 (1948).
(*Gordon v. Beck* (1925) 196 Cal. 768.)	*Gordon v. Beck*, 196 Cal. 768 (1925).

[a] Underscoring is used for illustrative purposes only to emphasize the spacing that distinguishes Bluebook abbreviations from those used by the California Style Manual.

§ 1:2   Abbreviations for official, unofficial, and regional reporters

General rule: The abbreviations for all case reporters (i.e., official, unofficial, and regional) are identical in both manuals. However, the Bluebook editors like more breathing room. They have inserted spaces between the abbreviation for the reporter and the series number. The only exception is the second series of the Pacific Reporter (i.e., there is no space between the abbreviation for the reporter and the series).

Cross-references: See generally Cal. Style Manual, Chapter 1. Bluebook, Table T.1, pp. 173–174.

Table 2
Official, Unofficial, and Regional Reporter Abbreviations

Official Case Reporter	California Style Manual	Bluebook
Supreme Court decisions (reported in the California Reports for the years 1950–1934)	Cal.	Cal.
(1934–1969)	Cal.2d	Cal._2d[a]
(1969–1991)	Cal.3d	Cal._3d
(1991–present)	Cal.4th	Cal._4th
Court of Appeal decisions (reported in the California Appellate Reports for the years 1905–1934)	Cal.App.	Cal._App.

Table 2—*Continued*

Official Case Reporter	California Style Manual	Bluebook
(1934–1969)	Cal.App.2d	Cal._App._2d
(1969–1991)	Cal.App.3d	Cal._App._3d
(1991–present)	Cal.App.4th	Cal._App._4th
Superior court appellate department decisions (bound with the California Appellate Reports for the years 1905–1934)	Cal.App.Supp.	Cal._App._Supp.
(1934–1969)	Cal.App.2d Supp.	Cal._App._2d Supp.
(1969–1991)	Cal.App.3d Supp.	Cal._App._3d Supp.

Unofficial Case Reporters	California Style Manual	Bluebook
Supreme Court, Court of Appeal, and superior court appellate department decisions (reported in the California Reporter for the years 1959–1991)	Cal.Rptr.	Cal._Rptr.
(1991–present)	Cal.Rptr.2d	Cal._Rptr._2d

Regional Case Reporters	California Style Manual	Bluebook
Supreme Court, Court of Appeal, and superior court appellate department decisions (reported in the Pacific Reporter for the years 1883–1931)	P.	P.
(1931–present)[b]	P.2d	P.2d

[a] Underscoring is used for illustrative purposes only to highlight the spacing that distinguishes Bluebook abbreviations from those used by the California Style Manual.

[b] In 1959, when the California Reporter was born, the Pacific Reporter stopped reporting the decisions of the California Court of Appeal.

§ 1:3 Parallel citations

General rule: In the California Style Manual, use of parallel citations is optional, but it is "the better practice" to use parallel citations when a case is first referenced. The title of the case is italicized or underscored, followed by the year in parentheses, and then the citation to the official reporter, followed by citations to the unofficial and regional reporters enclosed in brackets and ending with a period. The entire citation sentence is enclosed in parentheses unless it is an integral part of the sentence (i.e., deleting the citation would affect the meaning of the sentence).

In the Bluebook, when citing California Supreme Court decisions, parallel citations to the Pacific Reporter and to the California Reporter are required. The title of the case is italicized or underscored, followed by a comma and citations to the official reporter, the unofficial reporter, and the regional reporter separated by commas and followed by the year in parentheses. When citing all California Court of Appeal decisions and those of the lower courts, the Bluebook requires a parallel citation to either the Pacific Reporter (if the decision was rendered prior to 1959) or the California Reporter (if the decision was rendered in 1959 or later).

California Style Manual:

(*Mercy Hospital and Medical Center v. Farmers Insurance Group of Companies* (1997) 15 Cal.4th 213, 215 [61 Cal.Rptr.2d 638, 932 P.2d 210].)

(*Betts v. Allstate Insurance Company* (1984) 154 Cal.App.3d 688 [201 Cal.Rptr. 528].)

(*In re Trombley* (1948) 31 Cal.2d 801.)

Bluebook:

Mercy Hospital and Medical Center v. Farmers Insurance Group of Companies, 15 Cal. 4th 213, 215, 932 P.2d 210, 212, 61 Cal. Rptr. 2d 638, 640 (1997).

Betts v. Allstate Insurance Company, 154 Cal. App. 3d 688, 201 Cal. Rptr. 528 (1984).

In re Trombley, 31 Cal. 2d 801, 193 P.2d 734 (1948).

Brackets: The biggest difference regarding parallel citations is that the California Style Manual encloses citations to unofficial and regional reporters in brackets, while the Bluebook separates the citations with commas.

Point pages: When a citation refers to a specific quotation, holding, or dictum within a case, both manuals require the point page (i.e., the page on which the quotation, holding, or dictum appears) to be listed following the inception page of the official reporter citation. Point pages for parallel citations to the California Reporter are optional.

Order of citations: In the Bluebook, Pacific Reporter citations appear between the citation to the official reporter and the California Reporter; the California Style Manual places citations to the Pacific Reporter last.

Cross-references: Cal. Style Manual §§ 1:1[F], 1:12. Bluebook, Practitioners' Notes, P.3, pp. 34–35; Table T.1, p. 173.

Table 3
Parallel Citations

California Style Manual	Bluebook
(*Blue v. Los Angeles Unified School District* (1994) 26 Cal.App.4th Supp. 12 [31 Cal.Rptr.2d 923].)	*Blue v. Los Angeles Unified School District*, 26 Cal. App. 4th Supp. 12, 31 Cal. Rptr. 2d 923 (1994).
(*People v. Bloyd* (1987) 143 Cal.3d 333 [233 Cal.Rptr. 368, 729 P.2d 802].)	*People v. Bloyd*, 143 Cal. 3d 333, 729 P.2d 802, 233 Cal. Rptr. 368 (1987).
(*Eck v. McMichael* (1959) 176 Cal.App.2d 368 [1 Cal.Rptr. 369].)	*Eck v. McMichael*, 176 Cal. App. 2d 368, 1 Cal. Rptr. 369 (1959).

§ 1:4   Short form citations

General rule: The goal of short form citations is to provide sufficient information so that the reader may easily refer to the source without having to search back for the parent citation, yet be brief enough so that the shortened citation is not too distracting. Both manuals provide several options.

Repeat citation directly follows in same paragraph: In the California Style Manual, when the repeat citation directly follows the parent citation in the same paragraph, use "(*Ibid.*)" or "(*Id.* at p. ___)" instead of repeating the full citation. ("*Ibid.*" means "in the same place" and should only be used if the exact same citation is repeated.) If only the point page is different in the repeat citation, use "(*Id.* at p. ___)" instead.

In the Bluebook, when the repeat citation directly follows the parent citation in the same paragraph, use "*id.*" instead of repeating the full citation. If only the point page is different in the repeat citation, use "*Id.* at p." or "P.2d at" or "Cal. Rptr. at" and supply the point page instead of repeating the full citation.

California Style Manual:

Parent citation:

> (*Montrose Chemical Corp. v. Superior Court* (1993) 6 Cal.4th 287 [24 Cal.Rptr.2d 467, 861 P.2d 1153].)

Identical repeat citation directly following parent citation in same paragraph:

> (*Ibid.*)

Repeat citation with point page different than inception page, but directly following parent citation in same paragraph:

> (*Id.* at pp. 288–289.)

Bluebook:

Parent citation:

> *Montrose Chemical Corp. v. Superior Court*, 6 Cal. 4th 287, 861 P.2d 1153, 24 Cal. Rptr. 2d 467 (1993).

Identical repeat citation in same paragraph:

> *Id.*

Repeat citation with point page different from inception page:

> *Id.* at 288–89.

> *or* 861 P.2d at 1154.

> *or* 24 Cal. Rptr. 2d at 468.

Repeat citation does not directly follow, but is in same paragraph: In the California Style Manual, if the repeat citation does not directly follow the parent citation in the same paragraph, cite the full name of the case in italics followed by a comma, and then the volume number, the abbreviation for the official reporter, and "at p. ___." The entire citation sentence should be enclosed in parentheses. This rule applies to a repeat citation that appears in a string citation as well. It is also proper to omit the volume number and the reporter abbreviation. A third acceptable option is to simply cite the case by selecting one party's name (one that is not a common litigant, such as a governmental agency) followed by "at" and the page number.

In the Bluebook, if the repeat citation does not directly follow the parent citation in the same paragraph, cite the full name of the case in italics followed by a comma, the volume number, and the reporter abbreviation followed by "at p." and the point page. In the alternative, it is proper to omit the case name and cite solely to the volume number, reporter abbreviation, and "at p. ___."

California Style Manual:

Repeat citation in same paragraph, but not directly following parent citation:

(*Montrose Chemical Corp. v. Superior Court*, 6 Cal.4th at p. 288.)

or (*Montrose Chemical Corp. v. Superior Court* at p. 288.)

or (*Montrose Chemical Corp.* at p. 288.)

Bluebook:

Repeat citation in same paragraph, but not directly following parent citation:

Montrose Chemical Corp. v. Superior Court, 6 Cal. 4th at 288, 861 P.2d at 1154, 24 Cal. Rptr. 2d at 468.

or 6 Cal. 4th at 288, 861 P.2d at 1154, 24 Cal. Rptr. 2d at 468.

Repeat citation in different paragraph: In the California Style Manual, if the repeat citation appears in a different paragraph from the parent citation, cite the full case name in italics followed by the word "*supra*" and a comma, the volume number, the abbreviation for the official reporter in which it appears, and the page number on which the quotation, holding, or dictum appears. It is also proper to cite to one party's name, followed by a comma, the volume number, the abbreviation for the official reporter, and "at" followed by the page number.

In the Bluebook, if the repeat citation appears in a different paragraph from the parent citation, cite the name of one party (one that is not a common litigant, such as a governmental agency), followed by a comma, the volume number, the reporter abbreviation and "at ___." In the alternative, it is also proper to omit the case name altogether, and just cite to the volume number, the abbreviation of the official reporter, and "at ___," indicating the point page.

California Style Manual:

Repeat citation in different paragraph:

> (*Montrose Chemical Corp. v. Superior Court,* 6 Cal.4th at 288 [24 Cal.Rptr.2d at 468, 861 P.2d at 1154].)

> or (*Montrose Chemical Corp.,* 6 Cal.4th at 288 [24 Cal.Rptr.2d at 468, 861 P.2d at 1154].)

Bluebook:

Repeat citation in different paragraph:

> *Montrose Chemical,* 6 Cal. 4th at 288.

> or 6 Cal. 4th at 288.

"*Supra*": Only the California Style Manual uses "*supra*" to repeat a case citation in short form. "*Supra*" is, however, used in both manuals to cite secondary materials.

Short case names: Short case names alone are sometimes sufficient. After a case has been cited in full and its name repeated as part of the same general discussion, it is sufficient to use the short title of the case (e.g., "In *Betts*, the court noted . . .").

"*Ibid.*": Only use "*ibid.*" when using California Style Manual format and only where the repeat citation is identical in all respects to the parent citation (i.e., if the repeat citation contains a point page when the parent citation only included the inception page, it is not acceptable to use "*ibid.*"; use "*id.*").

Parallel citations: Both manuals require the inclusion of parallel citations.

Cross-references: Cal. Style Manual § 1:2[A]–[C]. Bluebook, Rule 4, p. 40.

Table 4
Rules Applicable to Short Form Citations

	California Style Manual	*Bluebook*
Parent citation:	(*Montrose Chemical Corp. v. Superior Court* (1993) 6 Cal.4th 287 [24 Cal.Rptr.2d 467, 861 P.2d 1153].)	*Montrose Chemical Corp. v. Superior Court*, 6 Cal. 4th 287, 861 P.2d 1153, 24 Cal. Rptr. 2d 467 (1993).
Repeat citation directly following parent citation in same paragraph:	(*Ibid.*)	*Id.*
Repeat citation in same paragraph as parent citation but different page number cited:	(*Id.* at p. 288.)	*Id.* at 288. or 861 P.2d at 1154. or 24 Cal. Rptr. 2d at 468.
Repeat citation in same paragraph following intervening citation or if parent citation appears in string citation:	(*Montrose Chemical Corp. v. Superior Court*, 6 Cal.4th at p. 288.) or (*Montrose Chemical Corp. v. Superior Court* at p. 288.) or (*Montrose Chemical Corp.* at p. 288.)	*Montrose Chemical Corp. v. Superior Court*, 6 Cal. 4th at 288, 861 P.2d at 1154, 24 Cal. Rptr. 2d at 468. or 6 Cal. 4th at 288, 861 P.2d at 1154, 24 Cal. Rptr. 2d at 468.
Repeat citation in different paragraph:	(*Montrose Chemical Corp. v. Superior Court*, 6 Cal.4th at 288, 24 Cal.Rptr.2d at p. 468, 861 P.2d at p. 1154.) or (6 Cal.4th at p. 288, 24 Cal.Rptr.2d at p. 468, 861 P.2d at p. 1154.)	*Montrose Chemical*, 6 Cal. 4th at 288. or 6 Cal. 4th at 288.

§ 1:5   Introductory signals

General rule: Signals such as "see," "see also," "see generally," "contra," "cf.," "accord," "compare," and "but see" are used in both manuals to introduce a citation and indicate in what way it is relevant to the preceding text or proposition; that is, to signal the reader that the authority cited directly or indirectly supports the preceding proposition or that it is contrary or analogous to it.

In both manuals, no signal is needed if the cited authority is directly referred to in the preceding text, such as in a quote.

California Style Manual:

As stated by the *Tunkle* court, "[n]o public policy opposes private, voluntary transactions in which one party, for a consideration, agrees to shoulder a risk that the law would otherwise have placed on the other party . . . ." (*Tunkle v. Regents of University of California* (1963) 60 Cal.2d 92, 101 [32 Cal.Rptr. 33, 383 P.2d 441] quoted in *Madison v. Superior Court* (1988) 203 Cal.App.3d 589, 598 [250 Cal.Rptr. 299].)

The signals "see also," "see generally," "cf.," "accord," and "compare" have the same meaning in both manuals.

Neither manual separates signals from case names with commas. Note that the Bluebook italicizes introductory signals (or underscores them) while the California Style Manual does not. However, if the introductory signal is used as a verb, as in the following example, not even the Bluebook italicizes:

California Style Manual:

See George K. Walker, *The Personification of the Vessel in United States Civil In Rem Actions and the International Law Context* (1991) 15 Tulane Maritime L.J. 177, for a discussion of vessel arrests and in rem jurisdiction.

Bluebook:

See George K. Walker, *The Personification of the Vessel in United States Civil In Rem Actions and the International Law Context,* 15 Tul. Mar. L.J. 177 (1991), for a discussion of vessel arrests and in rem jurisdiction.

California Style Manual:

(See *People v. Hines* (1997) 15 Cal.4th 997 [64 Cal.Rptr.2d 594, 938 P.2d 388].)

Bluebook:

See *People v. Hines,* 15 Cal. 4th 997, 938 P.2d 388, 64 Cal. Rptr. 2d 594 (1997).

Parenthetical explanations: The Bluebook recommends inserting parenthetical explanations when using "see also," "cf.," and "but cf." so that the relevance of the authority cited can be understood. The California Style Manual allows for parenthetical explanations as well but does not specifically recommend their use in connection with signals. (Cal. Style Manual § 1:4.) Parenthetical information should be included following the parallel citation and placed within the parentheses that enclose the citation sentence.

California Style Manual:

. . . and this conclusion is supported by *Shoemaker v. Myers* (1992) 2 Cal.App.4th 1407 [4 Cal.Rptr.2d 203] (where the court held that a *Tameny* claim accrues at the time an employee is terminated).)

Bluebook:

. . . and this conclusion is supported by *Shoemaker v. Myers,* 2 Cal. App. 4th 1407, 4 Cal. Rptr. 2d 203 (1992) (where the court held that a *Tameny* claim accrues at the time an employee is terminated).

Cross-references: Cal. Style Manual § 1:4. Bluebook, Rule 1.2, pp. 22–23.

Table 5
Using Introductory Signals

Signal	California Style Manual	Bluebook
Accord	Cited authority directly supports proposition stated in text but is from another jurisdiction; or two or more cited authorities directly support the proposition but only one is quoted in text.	Same

Table 5—*Continued*

Signal	California Style Manual	Bluebook
But cf.	None indicated.	Cited authority supports a proposition analogous to the contrary of the main proposition stated in the text
But see	Cited authority is dictum contrary to the main proposition stated in text.	Cited authority directly supports a proposition contrary to the one stated in the text
Cf.	Cited authority is analogous to proposition stated in text.	Same
Compare . . . with . . .	Cited authority contrasts the proposition stated in text.	Use "compare . . . with . . . [and] . . . with . . . [and] . . . "
Contra	Cited authority directly supports a proposition somewhat contrary or inconsistent with the one stated in text.	Use "but see" instead of "contra"
[No signal]	Cited authority directly supports proposition stated in text.	Same
See	Cited authority indirectly supports proposition stated in text or is dicta. If dicta, place "(dicta)" following the last page or point page.	Cited authority directly supports proposition stated in text
See also	Additional authority that generally supports proposition stated in text.	Same
See generally	Cited authority provides relevant background to proposition stated in text.	Same
See, e.g.,	Cited authorities are examples of proposition stated in text.	Same

§ 1:6   Punctuation separating authorities

General rule: Both manuals use semicolons to separate multiple authorities that follow the same signal.

California Style Manual:

(*Gray v. Zurich* (1966) 65 Cal.2d 263 [154 Cal.Rptr. 528, 419 P.2d 168];
    Betts v. Allstate Insurance Company (1984) 154 Cal.App.3d 688 [201
    Cal.Rptr. 528].)

Bluebook:

Gray v. Zurich, 65 Cal. 2d 263, 419 P.2d 168, 154 Cal. Rptr. 528 (1966);
    Betts v. Allstate Insurance Company, 154 Cal. App. 3d 688, 201 Cal.
    Rptr. 528 (1984).

Cross-references: Cal. Style Manual § 1:4. Bluebook, Rule 1.4, p. 25.

§ 1:7   Order of cited authority

General rule: Neither manual is rigid when it comes to the order in which citations appear. For example, the Bluebook provides that rules should be flexible and that a "substance-related rationale" should guide the author in establishing the order of citations. However, according to both manuals, citations should be listed in a manner that best supports the proposition for which they stand. Cases directly supporting the proposition are cited first. Cases indirectly supporting the proposition are cited second. Those containing dicta in accord are cited third; cases citing dicta in accord appear fourth; analogous cases appear fifth; cases with contrary holding appear sixth; and finally, cases with contrary dictum are cited last.

When multiple case citations are equally supportive of the proposition stated, the authority should appear in the following order: (1) constitutions and statutes, (2) case citations, and (3) secondary sources. More explicit instructions for citing authority in the proper order appear in Table 6 below.

Cross-references: Cal. Style Manual §§ 1.5[A]–[D], 2:5[C]. Bluebook, Rule 1.4, p. 25.

Table 6
Order of Authority

Order	California Style Manual	Bluebook
(1)	Constitutional citations	Constitutional citations (federal, state, and then foreign)
(2)	Code sections and statutes	Statutes and rules of evidence and procedure (federal, state (alphabetical by state), and then foreign (alphabetical by jurisdiction))
(3)	Case law: (a) United States Supreme Court cases (b) California Supreme Court cases (c) California Court of Appeal cases (d) federal court cases Within the foregoing order, cases should be prioritized by court level and then in reverse chronological order (i.e., with most recent case of the highest court listed first).	Treaties and other international agreements
(4)	Federal cases from other jurisdictions	Cases arranged in reverse chronological order (federal, state, foreign, and then international, all according to rank)
(5)	State cases from other jurisdictions in alphabetical order	Legislative materials
(6)	Secondary authorities	Administrative and executive materials
(7)		Resolutions, decisions, and regulations of intergovernmental organizations
(8)		Records, briefs, and petitions
(9)		Secondary materials

§ 1:8 Appendixes, comments, footnotes, pages, and the like

General rule: Abbreviations to appendixes, comments, footnotes, reporters' transcripts, sections, pages, and the like that appear in citations vary between the California Style Manual and the Bluebook and are illustrated in Table 7 below.

Cross-references: Cal. Style Manual §§ 1:8, 1:9, 2:33. Bluebook, Practitioners' Notes, P.7, p. 18; Rule 3.3(b), p. 35; Rule 3.5, pp. 38–39; Rule 12.8.5, pp. 84–85.

Table 7
Abbreviations for Appendixes, Comments, Footnotes, Pages, and the Like

Citing	California Style Manual	Bluebook
appendixes	"appen."	"app." or "app. at"
	Follows the inception page or point page, e.g., (*Madison v. Superior Court* (1988) 203 Cal.App.3d 589, 603, appen.).	E.g., *Madison v. Superior Court*, 203 Cal. App. 3d 589, app. at 603 (1988).
	Cal. Style Manual § 1:9	*Bluebook*, Rule 3.5, pp. 38–39
comments	"com.," "coms."	"cmt.," "cmts."
		E.g., *Restatement (Second) of Torts* § 623A cmt. a (1977).
	Cal. Style Manual §§ 2:33, 2:49	*Bluebook*, Rule 12.8.5, pp. 84–85
reporters' transcripts	"R.T."	"R."
		E.g., (2 R. at 17–18).
	Cal. Style Manual p. xxii	*Bluebook*, Practitioners' Notes, P.7, p. 18
footnotes	"fn."	"n.," "nn."
Where reference is to the footnote	E.g., (*Madison v. Superior Court* (1988) 203 Cal.App.3d 589, 593 fn. 1 [250 Cal.Rptr. 299].).	E.g., *Madison v. Superior Court*, 203 Cal. App. 3d 589, 593 n.1, 250 Cal. Rptr. 299 (1988). (No space between "n." and the footnote number.)
Where reference is to the footnote and the text	E.g., (*Madison v. Superior Court* (1988) 203 Cal.App.3d 589, 593 and fn. 1 [250 Cal. Rptr. 299].).	Same as above.
	Cal. Style Manual § 1:8	*Bluebook*, Rule 3.3(b), p. 35

Table 7—*Continued*

Citing	California Style Manual	Bluebook
pages	"p.," "pp."	Give the page number without any introductory abbreviation.
		Use "p." and "pp." only in internal cross-references.
	Cal. Style Manual §§ 2:8, 3:4, 3:10	*Bluebook*, Rule 3.3, pp. 34–35
paragraphs	"¶," "¶¶" *or* "par.," "pars."	"¶," "¶¶"
		E.g., 1 Blue Sky L. Rep. (CCH) ¶¶ 4471–4474.
		Spell out "paragraph" when it is the first word in a sentence.
	Cal. Style Manual § 2:8	*Bluebook*, Rule 6.2(b), p. 49
sections	"§," "§§" *or* "sec.," "secs."	"§," "§§"
	Use the singular with "et seq."	When citing consecutive sections, use inclusive numbers; do not use "et seq."
	With code abbreviations, use a comma preceding the section symbol or symbols.	Spell out "section" when it is the first word in a sentence.
	Cal. Style Manual § 2:6	*Bluebook*, Rule 3.4, pp. 37–38; Rule 6.2(b), p. 49
subdivisions	"subd.," "subds."	None.
	Use "subd." and "subds." with code abbreviations, e.g., (Civ. Code, § 2033, subds. (a)–(c).).	If citing several subsections within the *same* section, use only one section symbol; e.g., Cal. Civ. Code § 2033(a)–(c) (West 1998).
	Subdivision abbreviations are preceded by a comma.	If citing several subsections in *different* sections, use double section symbols; e.g., Cal. Civ. Code §§ 2033(a)–(c) and 2034(3)(e)(1) (West 1998).
	Cal. Style Manual § 2:7	*Bluebook*, Rule 3.4(b), pp. 37–38; Rule 6.2(b), p. 49

18

§ 1:9 Opinions from electronic sources

CD-ROM citations: If a case appears on a CD-ROM, the opinion will have a citation to at least the unofficial reporter, if not the official reporter. Both manuals follow standard rules of citation when citing a California opinion on a CD-ROM.

Westlaw and Lexis citations: These cases may be so recent as to not have an official or unofficial reporter citation.

In the California Style Manual, the case name reported by Westlaw or Lexis is cited in italics, followed by the date of the decision, a comma, and the docket number, all enclosed in parentheses, then the reporter abbreviation (with blanks left for the volume and page), the year of the decision and the Westlaw or Lexis citation enclosed in brackets. If the court issuing the decision is not readily identifiable from the citation, include an abbreviation for the name of the court inside the parentheses before the date.

In the Bluebook the italicized or underscored case name is followed by a comma, the abbreviation "No.," the docket number, and the Westlaw or Lexis citation (each separated by commas), then "at" and the screen or page number, and the abbreviation to the official reporter and date of decision in parentheses. Screen or page numbers should be preceded by an asterisk.

Aside from the usual differences (such as the use of parentheses and the placement of the date of decision), the Bluebook requires greater detail when citing a recent or unreported case, that is, the screen or page numbers preceded by an asterisk. The goal is to provide as much information as possible to enable the reader to locate the case and a point page, if relevant. The California Style Manual, on the other hand, does not require a screen page.

California Style Manual:

(In re Marriage of Butler & Gill (Mar. 11, 1997, D023944) ___ Cal.App.4th ___ [1997 WL 106434].)

(Maxwell v. Fire Insurance Exchange (Jan. 23, 1998, B101733) ___ Cal.App.4th ___ [1988 Lexis 56].)

Bluebook:

In re Marriage of Butler & Gill, No. D023944, 1997 WL 106434, at *1 (Cal. App. 4th Mar. 11, 1997).

Maxwell v. Fire Insurance Exchange, No. B101733, 1998 LEXIS 56, at *1 (Cal. App. 4th Jan. 23, 1998).

Internet citations: In the California Style Manual, the case name is in italics followed by the court, date of decision and document number in parentheses, followed by the reporter abbreviation (with blanks left for the volume and page), and then the Uniform Resource Locator or "URL," which is the Internet address on the World Wide Web for the case being cited.

In the Bluebook, citations to Internet sources are discouraged because of their transient nature. If the case is not in print, or it is difficult to find in its original form, citation to the Internet is allowed. However, there are no specific guidelines in the Bluebook for such citations. The example used below is consistent with the Bluebook style for citing articles and/or publications.

California Style Manual:

(*Santa Ana Food Market, Inc. v. Alcoholic Beverage Control Appeals Board* (November 29, 1999, No. G024485) ___ Cal.App.4th ___ <http://www.courtinfo.ca.gov/opinions/documents/G024485.PDF>.)

Bluebook:

Santa Ana Food Market, Inc. v. Alcoholic Beverage Control Appeals Board, No. G024485 (Cal. Ct. App. 4th Dist., November 29, 1999) <http://www.courtinfo.ca.gov/opinions/documents/G024485.PDF>.

Cross-references: Cal. Style Manual § 1:3. Bluebook, Rule 10.8.1(a), p. 68.

§ 1:10 Opinions from Daily Appellate Report and California Daily Opinion Service

General rule: Slip opinions of all California Supreme Court and Courts of Appeal decisions are reported in two daily services: the Los Angeles Daily Journal's or the San Francisco Daily Journal's Daily Appellate Report (D.A.R.) and the San Francisco Recorder's California Daily Opinion Service (C.D.O.S.). The slip opinions do not have an official citation; rather, they cite to the docket number, the date the decision was rendered, and the volume and identity of the issue in which they are printed. In the California Style Manual, the case name is cited in italics followed by the date of decision, a comma, and the docket number enclosed in parentheses, and then "___ Cal.App.4th ___," and in brackets, the volume number, the daily service reporter abbreviation and the page number. The entire citation is enclosed in parentheses. The Bluebook does not specifically address how to

cite D.A.R. or C.D.O.S., however, the examples below are generally in keeping with Bluebook citation style.

California Style Manual:

(*Bonds v. Roy* (March 31, 1998, G016807) ___ Cal.App.4th ___ [98 D.A.R.
4285].)

(*Taggares v. Superior Court (Mitchell)* (March 13, 1998, D027874) ___
Cal.App.4th ___ [98 C.D.O.S. 1878].)

Bluebook:

Bonds v. Roy, No. G016807, 98 D.A.R. 4285 (Cal. App. 4th March 31,
1998).

Taggares v. Superior Court (Mitchell), No. D027874, 98 C.D.O.S. 1878
(Cal. App. 4th March 13, 1998).

Cross-references: Cal. Style Manual § 1:17[B]. See generally Bluebook, Rule 10.8.1, pp. 68–69; Rule 18.1, p. 129.

§ 1:11 Decisions of the superior court appellate departments

General rule: Opinions of the appellate departments of California
superior courts are reported in the California Appellate Reports in a separate section or supplement to the Court of Appeal decisions. Both manuals
use the identifying term "Supp." following the abbreviation for the reporter.
Aside from the customary differences concerning parentheses, the use of
brackets, and the placement of the year, the format utilized by both manuals
is standard.

California Style Manual:

(*Blue v. Los Angeles Unified School District* (1994) 26 Cal.App.4th Supp.
12 [31 Cal.Rptr.2d 923].)

(*People v. Murphy* (1998) 61 Cal.App.4th Supp. 5 [___ Cal.Rptr.2d ___].)

Bluebook:

Blue v. Los Angeles Unified School District, 26 Cal. App. 4th Supp. 12, 31
Cal. Rptr. 2d 923 (1994).

People v. Murphy, 61 Cal. App. 4th Supp. 5, ___ Cal. Rptr. 2d ___ (1998).

Advance sheet opinions: Advance sheet opinions for the appellate
departments of the superior court are reported in advance pamphlets. In the

California Style Manual, the standard rules of citation are followed. The only difference is that the pamphlet number ("pamp. No.") in which the sheet opinion appears is the last "phrase" of the citation sentence. The Bluebook does not address this California-specific item, however, the example used below is in keeping with general Bluebook style.

California Style Manual:

(*Lim v. Silverton* (1997) 61 Cal.App.4th Supp. 1, pamp. No. 8.)

Bluebook:

Lim v. Silverton, 61 Cal. App. 4th Supp. 1, pamp. No. 8 (1997).

Cross-references: Cal. Style Manual § 1:15. See generally Bluebook, Rule 10.8.1, pp. 68–69.

§ 1.12 Trial court cases

General rule: The California Style Manual places the case name in italics or underscoring, and follows it with the court, county, year of decision, and the docket number enclosed in parentheses. The entire citation sentence is enclosed in parentheses, as is customary.

The Bluebook does not address superior court case opinions. However, the standard Bluebook citation form suggests citation to the case name (with italics or underscoring), the docket number, and followed by the court, county, and year of decision.

California Style Manual:

(*Schnepf v. Childs & Sons et al.* (Super. Ct. San Diego County, 1997, No. 715556.)

(*Corso v. Scuba Duba Dive Shop et al.* (Super. Ct. L.A. County, 1984, No. 021243.)

Bluebook:

Schnepf v. Childs & Sons et al., No. 715556 (Super. Ct. San Diego County 1997) .

Corso v. Scuba Duba Dive Shop et al., No. 021243 (Super. Ct. L.A. County 1984).

Cross-references: Cal. Style Manual § 1:16. See generally Bluebook, Rule 10.8.1, pp. 68–69.

CHAPTER 1
—Notes—

CHAPTER 1
—Notes—

CHAPTER 2

CALIFORNIA OPINIONS: CITING PROCEDURAL PHASES AND SUBSEQUENT AND PRIOR CASE HISTORY

§ 2:1   Cases pending in appellate court

General rule: In the California Style Manual, the docket number and other material concerning the procedural posture of the case must be included in the citation. The examples in the California Style Manual vary in terms of the placement of the docket number, the procedural history, and relevant date, giving rise to the inference that no particular sequence is required.

In the Bluebook, pending cases are cited by the case name (in italics or underscored), followed by a comma and the docket number prefaced with the abbreviation "No." Immediately following the docket number, enclose the court, the relevant date (if not otherwise explained), and the procedural history in parentheses.

California Style Manual:

Sampson v. Gilliam (D031836) is scheduled for oral argument on December 13, 1999, before our Court of Appeal for the Fourth District.

This issue will no doubt be resolved by *Farmers' Rice Cooperative v. Workers' Comp. Appeals Board* (C032667), which is currently pending.

(*Elliott v. County of El Dorado* (C032396, app. pending).)

Bluebook:

Sampson v. Gilliam, No. D031836, is scheduled for oral argument on
    December 13, 1999, before the California Court of Appeal for the
    Fourth District.

This issue will no doubt be resolved by *Farmers' Rice Cooperative v.
    Workers' Comp. Appeals Board,* No. C032667 (Cal. Ct. App. 4th Dist.
    1999), which is currently pending.

Elliott v. County of El Dorado, No. C032396 (Cal. Ct. App. 3d Dist., 1999)
    appeal docketed.

Italics: The Bluebook italicizes explanatory phrases such as "review
granted" or "reh'g granted." The California Style Manual does not.

Abbreviations: Abbreviations of explanatory phrases describing the
procedural phase of a case differ between the manuals to some extent. For
example, note the abbreviation for "rehearing" in the examples shown in
Table 8 below. A complete list of abbreviations for explanatory phrases in
both manuals appears in Table 9 in § 2:3.

Cross-references: Cal. Style Manual § 1:17. Bluebook, Rule 10.5(c),
p. 65; Rule 10.8.1(b), p. 69.

Table 8
Citations to Cases Pending in Appellate Court

California Style Manual	Bluebook
(Hoff v. Vacaville Unified School Dist. (S050162, review granted March 11, 1998).)	*Hoff v. Vacaville Unified School Dist.,* No. S050162 (*review granted* March 11, 1998).
(Shapiro v. Sutherland (B103078, rehg. granted Feb. 2, 1998).)	*Shapiro v. Sutherland,* No. B103078 (*reh'g granted* Feb. 2, 1998).
(Landau v. Superior Court (S068095, review granted April 15, 1998, further action deferred pending disposition of *Leone v. Medical Board,* S065485, or further order of the court).)	*Landau v. Superior Court,* No. S068095 (*review granted* April 15, 1998, further action deferred pending disposition of *Leone v. Medical Board,* No. S065485, or further order of the court).

§ 2:2   Modified opinions

General rule: Opinions may be modified prior to their publication in bound volumes. Modifications are published in the advance sheets or pamphlets. By the time the bound volume is published, the modification will be incorporated into the initial decision.

In the California Style Manual, the following guidelines apply: If a modification is short, it will appear in the back of the next available advance pamphlet on "a," "b," "c," etc. pages. Until the modification is merged with the initial decision and published as modified in the bound volumes, it should be cited to page "a," "b," "c," etc. following the initial citation. Modifications need only be cited if they are relevant to the proposition stated in the text that the citation supports.

If a modification to an opinion is extensive, the opinion will be republished as modified and will bear a citation different from the earlier opinion. In such case, cite the advance sheet containing the republication, with no mention of the earlier publication.

The Bluebook does not address modifications with any specificity (other than to indicate that the terms "modifying" and "modified" should appear in italics and should not be abbreviated). The example below is generally in keeping with Bluebook style.

California Style Manual:

(*Western Digital Corp. v. Superior Court* (1998) 60 Cal.App.4th 1471, mod. 61 Cal.App.4th 471a.)

Bluebook:

Western Digital Corp. v. Superior Court, 60 Cal. App. 4th 1471, *modified,* 61 Cal. App. 4th 471a (1998).

Cross-references: Cal. Style Manual § 1:20. Bluebook, Table T.9, p. 292.

§ 2:3   Subsequent history in citations

General rule: Both manuals provide that the subsequent history of a case should be cited when it is significant to the point for which the case is cited. In addition, both manuals suggest that the subsequent history be appended to the primary citation and prefaced with an appropriate explanatory word or phrase such as "vacated as moot," "judgment vacated," "rehearing granted," or the like. For a list of explanatory words and phrases describing an opinion's history and commonly used abbreviations, see Table 9 on page 29.

Both manuals discourage including denials of certiorari or denials of discretionary appeals in a case's subsequent history. The Bluebook indicates that it is permissible only where the case is less than two years old or if the denial is particularly relevant to the discussion.

Consistent with California Rules of Court, rules 976(d) and 977, the California Style Manual prohibits reliance on a Court of Appeal opinion that is pending in the Supreme Court, or where the Supreme Court has granted review. This general rule is subject to the exceptions set forth in rule 977(b). After the Supreme Court has rendered a decision, the Court of Appeal opinion is considered unpublished (unless ordered otherwise). If ordered published by the court, the Court of Appeal opinion is re-reported in the California Reports with the case history. The original citation of the Court of Appeal opinion is superseded by the number assigned to the re-reported opinion.

California Style Manual:

(*Natural Milk Producers Assn. v. City and County of San Francisco* (1942) 20 Cal.2d 101 [124 P.2d 25], vacated as moot on federal question in (1943) 317 U.S. 423 [63 S.Ct. 359, 87 L.Ed. 375], and readopted in (1944) 24 Cal.2d. 122 [148 P.2d 377].)

(*California Teachers Assn. v. Governing Board of Rialto Unified School District* (1997) 14 Cal.4th 627 [59 Cal.Rptr.2d 671, 927 P.2d 1175], judgment vacated (1996) 45 Cal.App.4th 223 [47 Cal.Rptr.2d 795].)

(*Kentucky Fried Chicken of Cal. Inc. v. Superior Court* (1997) 14 Cal.4th 814 [59 Cal.Rptr.2d 756, 927 P.2d 1260], review granted (1996) 49 Cal.App.4th 167 [47 Cal.Rptr.2d 69].)

Bluebook:

Natural Milk Producers Ass'n v. City and County of San Francisco, 20 Cal. 2d 101, 124 P.2d 25 (1942), *vacated as moot on federal question in* 317 U.S. 423, 63 S. Ct. 359, 87 L. Ed. 375 (1943) *and readopted in* 24 Cal. 2d 122, 148 P.2d 377 (1944).

California Teachers Ass'n v. Governing Board of Rialto Unified School District, 14 Cal. 4th 627, 927 P.2d 1175, 59 Cal. Rptr. 2d 671 (1997), *judgment vacated*, 45 Cal. App. 4th 223, 47 Cal. Rptr. 2d 795 (1996).

Kentucky Fried Chicken of Cal. Inc v. Superior Court, 14 Cal. 4th 814, 927 P.2d 1260, 59 Cal. Rptr. 756 (1997), *review granted*, 49 Cal. App. 4th 167, 47 Cal. Rptr. 2d 69 (1996).

Italics: In the Bluebook, explanatory words or phrases used to describe an opinion's history are italicized. In contrast, the California Style Manual does not use italics, except for the abbreviations "*sub nom.*" and "*per curiam.*"

Commas: The Bluebook alone uses commas to separate explanatory phrases from the appended citation. The only time commas are not used is where the explanatory phrase ends with a preposition (e.g., "certifying questions to," "dismissing appeal from," or "overruled by") and following active verbs such as "enforcing," "rev'g," or "vacating as moot."

Abbreviations: Abbreviations of the words commonly used to describe an opinion's history vary between the California Style Manual and the Bluebook. For a comparison, see Table 9 below.

Cross-references: Cal. Style Manual § 1:11, and see § 1:17. Bluebook, Rule 10.7, p. 66; Rule 10.7.1, pp. 66–67; Table T.9, p. 292.

Table 9
Abbreviations of Explanatory Words or Phrases for Subsequent History

Descriptor	California Style Manual	Bluebook
affirmed	affd.	*aff'd,*
affirmed by an equally divided court	affd. by an equally divided court,	*aff'd by an equally divided court,*
affirmed by memorandum opinion	affd. mem.	*aff'd mem.,*
affirmed under the name of	affd. *sub nom.*	*aff'd sub nom.*
affirmed on other grounds	[none given]	*aff'd on other grounds,*
affirmed on rehearing	[none given]	*aff'd on reh'g*

Table 9—*Continued*

Descriptor	California Style Manual	Bluebook
affirming	[none given]	*aff'g*
acquittal	[none given]	*acq.*
acquittal in result	[none given]	*acq. in result*
amended by	amended by	*amended by*
appeal denied	app. denied	*appeal denied,*
appeal dismissed	app. dism.	*appeal dismissed,*
appeal docketed	app. docketed	*appeal docketed,*
appeal filed	app. filed	*appeal filed,*
appeal pending	app. pending	*appeal pending,*
argued	argued	*argued,*
certiorari denied	cert. den.	*cert. denied,*
certiorari dismissed	[none given]	*cert. dismissed,*
certiorari granted	cert. granted	*cert. granted,*
certifying questions to	[none given]	*certifying questions to*
concurring	conc.	[none given]
Court of Appeal	Ct. App.	[none given]
denied	den.	[none given]
denying certiorari to	[none given]	*denying cert. to*
dismissed	dism.	[none given]
dismissed per stipulation	dism. per stip.	[none given]
dismissing appeal from	[none given]	*dismissing appeal from*
dissenting	dis.	[none given]
effective	eff.	[none given]

Table 9—*Continued*

Descriptor	California Style Manual	Bluebook
enforced	[none given]	*enforced,*
enforcing	[none given]	*enforcing,*
following	foll.	[none given]
hearing denied	hg. den.	[none given]
hearing granted	hg. granted	[none given]
improvidently	improv.	[none given]
instructions	Instns.	[none given]
majority	maj.	[none given]
mandamus denied	[none given]	*mandamus denied,*
modified	mod.	*modified,*
modifying	[none given]	*modifying,*
nonacquittal	[none given]	*nonacq.*
nonpublished	nonpub.	[none given]
opinion	opn.	[none given]
overruled by	[none given]	*overruled by*
partially published	par. pub.	[none given]
petition	petn.	[none given]
petition for certiorari filed	[none given]	*petition for cert. filed,*
plurality	plur.	[none given]
probable jurisdiction noted	prob. jur. noted	*prob. juris. noted,*
published	pub.	[none given]
rehearing denied	rehg. denied	*reh'g denied,*
rehearing granted	rehg. granted	*reh'g granted,*

Table 9—*Continued*

Descriptor	California Style Manual	Bluebook
retransferred	retrans.	[none given]
reversed	revd.	*rev'd,*
reversed on other grounds	[none given]	*rev'd on other grounds,*
reversed per curiam	revd. *per curiam*	*rev'd per curiam,*
reversing	revg.	*rev'g*
review denied	review den.	[none given]
review granted	review granted	[none given]
stipulation	stip.	[none given]
Supreme Court	Supreme Ct.	[none given]
transferred	trans.	[none given]
under the name of	*sub nom.*	*sub nom.*
vacated	vacated	*vacated,*
vacating as moot	[none given]	*vacating as moot*
withdrawn	[none given]	*withdrawn,*

§ 2:4   Prior history in citations

General rule: The California Style Manual does not distinguish between citing prior and subsequent history. For further discussion, see § 2:3 of this guide.

The Bluebook, however, prescribes the use of prior case history *only* where it is "significant" (versus "relevant") to the point for which a case is cited. Logically enough, the Bluebook requires that the prior history appear before the subsequent history of the case.

Cross-references: Cal. Style Manual §§ 1:11, 1:17. Bluebook, Rule 10.7, p. 66; Rule 10.7.1(a), p. 67.

CHAPTER 2
—Notes—

CHAPTER 2
—Notes—

CHAPTER 3

CALIFORNIA ADMINISTRATIVE AGENCY AND APPEALS BOARD DECISIONS

§ 3:1   Citations to administrative agency and appeals board decisions

General rule: The California Style Manual is the only manual of style that specifically addresses how to cite California administrative agencies and appeals board decisions. It is preferable to cite the official compilation of the administrative decisions or, if none is available, the topical reporter or an electronic source. If citing an official compilation, a parallel citation to the topical reporter, enclosed in brackets, may also be included. (See generally § 1:3 of this guide.)

Aside from Westlaw and Lexis reporting the agencies' decisions soon after they are filed, some state agencies post their decisions on their own Web sites. (See § 1:9.)

The Bluebook recommends citing state administrative and executive materials by analogy to the federal examples given. All Bluebook examples in the sections that follow are in keeping with this suggested format.

Cross-references: Cal. Style Manual §§ 1:22–1:24. Bluebook, Rule 14, p. 93; Table T.1, pp. 173–175.

§ 3:2   Agricultural Labor Relations Board decisions

General rule: Agricultural Labor Relations Board decisions are published annually and numbered sequentially. Decisions in the bound volumes are not paginated consecutively; for that reason, point pages are to the filed decisions.

In the California Style Manual, the name of the matter or the full reported name of the first-listed private party is italicized, the date of the decision follows in parentheses, then the volume number, the abbreviations "ALRB" and "No.," followed by the number of the decision, and the point page (if relevant). As is customary, the entire citation sentence is enclosed in parentheses.

In the Bluebook, the name of the matter or the full reported name of the first-listed private party is italicized or underscored, followed by a comma, the volume number, the abbreviations "A.L.R.B." and "No." followed by the number of the decision, and ending with the date of the decision in parentheses.

California Style Manual:

(*Warmerdam Packing Co.* (1998) 24 ALRB No. 2, p. 3.)

Bluebook:

Warmerdam Packing Co., 24 A.L.R.B. No. 2, p. 3 (1998).

Cross-references: Cal. Style Manual § 1:22[E]. Bluebook, Rules 14.3–14.3.1(a), pp. 95–96.

§ 3:3   Attorney General opinions

General rule: In the California Style Manual, Attorney General opinions are cited by volume number, the abbreviation "Ops.Cal.Atty.Gen.," the page number, and then the year of the opinion in parentheses. Advance sheets bear the same pagination as the bound volumes so they are indistinguishable (e.g., "81 Ops.Cal.Atty.Gen. 1 (1998)," cited below, is an advance sheet opinion). As is customary, the California Style Manual encloses the citation sentence in parentheses except when the citation forms an integral part of the sentence.

In the Bluebook, the sequence of citation is identical to that of the California Style Manual. However, the abbreviation for the official reporter is "Op. Cal. Att'y Gen."

California Style Manual:

(81 Ops.Cal.Atty.Gen. 1 (1998).)

(81 Ops.Cal.Atty.Gen. 1, 3–4 (1998).)

The issue of whether the proposed merger between Pacific Enterprises and Enora Corporation would adversely affect competition was addressed in 81 Ops.Cal.Atty.Gen. 1 (1998).

Bluebook:

81 Op. Cal. Att'y Gen. 1 (1998).

81 Op. Cal. Att'y Gen. 1, 3–4 (1998).

The issue of whether the proposed merger between Pacific Enterprises and Enora Corporation would adversely affect competition was addressed in 81 Op. Cal. Att'y Gen. 1 (1998).

Cross-references: Cal. Style Manual § 1:23. Bluebook, Rule 14.4, p. 97.

§ 3:4   California Workers' Compensation Appeals Board cases

General rule: Opinions of the California Workers' Compensation Appeals Board are currently reported in California Compensation Cases (Cal.Comp.Cases). Prior to 1936, they were reported in the Decisions of the Industrial Accident Commission (I.A.C.). Citations to opinions from these reports are illustrated below. Note the difference between the reporter abbreviations.

California Style Manual:

(*Ford v. Lawrence Berkeley Laboratory* (1997) 62 Cal.Comp.Cases 479.)

(*Macy's of California v. Workers' Compensation Appeals Board* (1998) 63 Cal.Comp.Cases 872.)

Bluebook:

Ford v. Lawrence Berkeley Laboratory, 62 Cal. Workers' Comp. C. 479 (1997).

Macy's of California v. Workers' Compensation Appeals Board, 63 Cal. Workers' Comp. C. 872 (1998).

Unofficial reporter: Summaries of workers' compensation cases (such as panel decisions denying reconsideration) are published in the unofficial California Workers' Compensation Reporter (Cal. Workers' Comp. Rptr.) and aside from the customary citation format, should include the docket number as illustrated below:

California Style Manual:

(*Snyder v. Michael's Stores, Inc.* (1997) SO57064, 62 Cal. Workers' Comp. Rptr. 1351.)

Bluebook:

Snyder v. Michael's Stores, Inc., No. SO57064, 62 Cal. Workers' Comp. Rep. 1351 (1997).

Cross-references: Cal. Style Manual § 1:22[B]. Bluebook, Rule 14.3, p. 95; Table T.7, p. 289.

§ 3:5   Fair Employment and Housing Commission precedential decisions

General rule: In the California Style Manual, Fair Employment and Housing Commission (Dept. Fair Empl. & Hous.) decisions are identified by case name (in italics or underscored), followed by the date of decision in parentheses, the decision number, a comma, the abbreviations "FEHC" and "Precedential Decs." (if relevant), then the abbreviation "CEB" for the California Continuing Education of the Bar binder in which the decision appears, followed by a comma, the abbreviation "p.," and then the page number.

In the Bluebook, Fair Employment and Housing Commission decisions are identified by the full reported name of the first-listed party, the abbreviations "F.E.H.C." and "Precedential Dec. No." (if relevant), the decision number, and the year of the decision in parentheses.

California Style Manual:

(*Dept. Fair Empl. & Hous. v. Nancy A. Konig* (September 13, 1998) FEHC Dec. No. 98-06, CEB 5, p. 1.)

(*Dept. Fair Empl. & Hous. v. McWay Family Trust* (1996) No. 96-07, FEHC Precedential Decs. 1996–1997, CEB 1, p. 2.)

In *Dept. Fair Empl. & Hous. v. Stevan Jevremov* (1997) FEHC Dec. No. 97-02, CEB 1, pages 5 to 6, the commission held . . .

Bluebook:

Nancy A. Konig, F.E.H.C. Dec. No. 9702 (1997).

McWay Family Trust, F.E.H.C. Precedential Dec. No. 96-07 (1996).

Stevan Jevremov, F.E.H.C. Dec. 97-02 (1997).

Cross-references: Cal. Style Manual § 1:22[G]. Bluebook, Rule 14.1, p. 93; Rule 14.3.1(a), p. 95; but cf. Table T.1, pp. 168–169.

§ 3:6   Public Employment Relations Board decisions

General rule: Decisions of the Public Employment Relations Board (PERB) are distributed in typescript exactly as they are filed by the charging party. The Public Employee Reporter for California (PERC), an unofficial reporter, annotates and publishes the decisions and has a wider distribution than the official publications. Therefore, parallel citations to PERC should be included.

In the California Style Manual, the name of the respondent appears in italics or underscored, the year of the decision in parentheses, followed by the abbreviation "PERB Dec. No." for PERB decision number, the number of the decision and, in brackets, the parallel citation to PERC. The parallel citation should be to the volume and paragraph number where the decision appears, along with any point page number.

California Style Manual:

(*Sonoma County Office of Education* (1998) PERB Dec. No. 1289-S [16 PERC ¶ 23003, p. 310].)

(Trustees of the California State University v. Academic Professionals of California (1997) PERB Dec. No. 1150 [22 PERC ¶ 29001].)

Bluebook:

Sonoma County Office of Education, P.E.R.B. Dec. No. 1289-S at 226, 16 P.E.R.C. ¶ 23003 at 310 (1998).

Trustees of the California State University v. Academic Professionals of California, P.E.R.B. Dec. No. 1150 at 102, 22 P.E.R.C. ¶ 29001 at 9 (1997).

Cross-references: Cal. Style Manual § 1:22[F]. Cf. Bluebook, Table T.1, p. 169.

§ 3:7   Public Utilities Commission and California Railroad Commission decisions

General rule: In 1946, the California Railroad Commission (C.R.C.) became the California Public Utilities Commission (Cal.P.U.C.). Now in its second series, publication of Cal.P.U.C.2d was suspended in 1983 at volume 10 and resumed in 1989. Following are examples of citations to the commission's decisions:

California Style Manual:

(Arrowhead Manor Water Co. (1946) 46 C.R.C. 656.)

(Twin Lake Enterprises, Inc. (1995) 63 Cal.P.U.C.2d 112.)

Bluebook:

Arrowhead Manor Water Co., 46 C.R.C. 656 (1946).

Twin Lake Enterprises, Inc., 63 Cal. P.U.C. 2d 112 (1995).

Cross-references: Cal. Style Manual § 1:22[D]. Cf. Bluebook, Table T.7, p. 288.

§ 3:8   State Board of Equalization decisions

California Style Manual:

(Appeal of Gasco Gasoline, Inc. (1988) 88 SBE 017 [Cal. Tax. Rptr. (CCH) ¶ 23003, at p. 1].)

Bluebook:

Appeal of Gasco Gasoline, Inc., 88 Cal. S.B.E. 017, Cal. Tax. Rep. (CCH) ¶
   23003 at 1 (1988).

Cross-references: Cal. Style Manual § 1:22[C]. Cf. Bluebook, Table
T.15, p. 324.

§ 3:9   State Bar Court decisions

California Style Manual:

(In the Matter of Katz (Review Dept. 1995) 3 Cal. State Bar Ct. Rptr. 430.)

Bluebook:

In the Matter of Katz, 3 Cal. State Bar Ct. Rep. 430 (Review Dep't 1995).

Cross-references: Cal. Style Manual § 1:24. Bluebook, Rule 14.3,
pp. 95–96.

CHAPTER 3
—Notes—

CHAPTER 4

CITING OUT-OF-STATE OPINIONS
IN CALIFORNIA STATE COURTS

§ 4:1   Citations to out-of-state opinions

Initial citations: In the California Style Manual, an out-of-state opinion cited for the first time must include the official state reporter and a parallel citation to a regional reporter in the National Reporter System. The format of the citation is identical to that used when citing California case law.

In the Bluebook, initial references to out-of-state court opinions must be to the regional reporter citation or to the official state reporter, if available, or to another unofficial reporter.

Repeat citations: In the California Style Manual, repeat citations to out-of-state opinions should be to regional reporter. Inclusion of the official state reporter cite is optional.

In the Bluebook, no special treatment of repeat citations to out-of-state opinions is mentioned. (See § 1:4 of this guide.)

Reminder: Trial courts require a copy of out-of-state authority. Rule 313(e) of the California Rules of Court requires that counsel attach a copy of any out-of-state authority relied on in their memorandum of points and authorities to their moving papers.

Cross-references: Cal. Style Manual § 1:28. Bluebook, Rule 10.3.1(b), p. 61; Rule 10.4(b), p. 64.

Table 10
Citing Opinions from Other States

California Style Manual	Bluebook
(Rebenolt v. Chrysler Financial Services Corp. (1991) 201 Ga.App. 168 [410 S.E.2d. 365].)	*Rebenolt v. Chrysler Financial Services Corp.*, 201 Ga. App. 168, 410 S.E. 2d 365 (1991).
(Aloha Unlimited Inc. v. Coughlin (Hawaii App. 1995) 904 P.2d 541.)	*Aloha Unlimited Inc. v. Coughlin*, 904 P.2d 541 (Haw. App. 1995).
(Plourde v. Plourde (Me. 1996) 678 A.2d 1032.)	*Plourde v. Plourde*, 678 A.2d 1032 (Me. 1996).
(Washburn v. Beatt Equipment Co. (1992) 120 Wash.2d 246 [840 P.2d 860].)	*Washburn v. Beatt Equipment Co.*, 120 Wash. 2d 246, 840 P.2d 860 (1992).
(Kendall v. Selvagglio (1992) 413 Mass. 619 [602 N.E.2d 206].)	*Kendall v. Sevlagglio*, 413 Mass. 619, 602 N.E.2d 206 (1992).

§ 4:2   Abbreviations for state and regional reporters

General rule: Neither manual abbreviates the names of the reporters of Alaska, Idaho, Iowa, Ohio, or Utah. In both manuals, the abbreviations used for all other state and regional reporters are identical except for those of Hawaii and Washington.

In the California Style Manual, "Hawaii" is not abbreviated. In the Bluebook, it is abbreviated as "Haw." In the California Style Manual, the abbreviation "Wash." applies only to the first series of Washington Reports. The second series is abbreviated as "Wn.2d," and Washington Appellate Reports as "Wn.App."

There are also several exceptions relating to spaces. The California Style Manual closes up spaces in "Cal.Rptr.," "Cal.Rptr.2d," and "So.2d," while Bluebook style is to leave them open.

California Style Manual:

Cal.Rptr.

Cal.Rptr.2d

Hawaii

So.2d

Wn.2d

Wn.App.

Bluebook:

Cal. Rptr.

Cal. Rptr. 2d

Haw.

So. 2d

Wash. 2d

Wash. App.

Cross-references: Cal. Style Manual § 1:30[A]. Bluebook, Table T.10, p. 293.

CHAPTER 4
—Notes—

CHAPTER 5
CALIFORNIA CONSTITUTION, CODES, REGULATIONS, AND RULES

§ 5:1   Citations to California Constitution

General rule: In the California Style Manual, citations to the California Constitution begin with the abbreviation "Cal. Const." followed by the abbreviation "art." for article, the article number, a comma, the relevant section, and if appropriate, reference to a particular clause. As with case cites, the citation is enclosed in parentheses unless it forms an integral part of the sentence. No abbreviations are used for citations that are not included in parentheses. Moreover, the words "state" and "California" may be omitted from citations outside parentheses where it is clear from the text that the citation refers to the California Constitution.

In the Bluebook, the format of citations to the California Constitution is nearly identical to that of the California Style Manual. The Bluebook, however, uses fewer commas (i.e., only to separate the article number from the section symbol).

Short form citations to the California Constitution: In the Bluebook, the only short form for citing a constitutional amendment is "*id.*" The California Style Manual has no such requirement.

California Style Manual:

(Cal. Const., art. I, § 2(a).)

For the constitutional demarcation of the separation of governmental powers, refer to article III, section 3 of the California Constitution.

Property owned by the State is exempt from property taxation (Cal. Const., art. 13, § 3(a)).

(Cal. Const., art. XIII, § 28, subd. (f), par. (3).)

Bluebook:

Cal. Const. art. I, § 2(a).

For the constitutional demarcation of the separation of governmental powers, refer to art. III, § 3 of the Cal. Const.

Property owned by the State is exempt from property taxation (Cal. Const. art. 13, § 3(a)).
Cal. Const. art. XIII, § 28(f)(3).

Cross-references: Cal. Style Manual § 2:3. Bluebook, Rule 11, p. 73.

§ 5:2 Citations to California codes in main volumes

In the California Style Manual, if a sentence begins with a discussion of a particular code section, such as "Sections 11430.20 and 11430.21 of the Government Code provide . . . ," no abbreviations are allowed. Every word in the citation (e.g., "section," "article," "subdivision") is spelled out. Likewise, if the code section is an integral part of the sentence in which it appears, no abbreviations are used. (See § 5:3 below for discussion of when abbreviations are allowed.)

In the Bluebook, the first word of every sentence must be spelled out. Hence, if a sentence begins with a discussion of section 437c of the California Code of Civil Procedure, the word "section" must be spelled out. All

California code titles are prefaced with the abbreviation "Cal." (See Table 11 in § 5:8 for a list of code title abbreviations.) A section symbol follows the title (rather than the word "section") and then the section number. The citation ends with the name of the publisher (e.g., Deering or West) and the year of publication in parentheses.

California Style Manual:

Code of Civil Procedure section 437c was last revised in 1994.

Section 437c, subdivision (a) of the Code of Civil Procedure was last revised in 1994.

California's Attachment Law is set forth in Civil Code section 481.010 et seq.

Penal Code section 13860 et seq. contain the . . .

(Civ. Code, § 538.)

Bluebook:

Cal. Civ. Proc. Code § 437c (Deering 1995) was last revised in 1994.

Section 437c(a) of Cal. Civ. Proc. Code (West Supp. 1998) was last revised in 1994.

California's Attachment Law is set forth in Cal. Civ. Proc. Code §§ 482.010–493.060 (West 1979).

Cal. Penal Code §§ 13860–13864 contain the . . .

Cal. Civ. Code § 538 (West 1999).

Cross-references: Cal. Style Manual § 2:6. Bluebook, Rule 6.2(b), p. 49.

§ 5:3   Code citation sentences

General rule: In the California Style Manual, abbreviations are used for the titles of codes in citations enclosed in parentheses. In such cases, the code abbreviation is followed by a comma, a section symbol and the section number.

In the Bluebook, the format for citing code sections is the same regardless of whether the citation is included within a sentence or appears after it.

California Style Manual:

(Code Civ. Proc., § 437c, subd. (b).)

(Code Civ. Proc, § 482.010 et seq.)

(Gov. Code, § 11430.20, art. 7, subd. (a) & (b).)

(Pen. Code, §§ 1000, 1000.12.)

Bluebook:

Cal. Civ. Proc. Code § 437c(b).

Cal. Civ. Proc. Code §§ 481.010–493.060 (West 1979).

Cal. Gov. Code § 11430.20, article 7, subdivision (a) (West Supp. 1998).

Cal. Penal Code §§ 1000, 1000.1 (Deering 1998).

Titles: Unlike case titles, code titles are not underscored or italicized in either manual.

Year and publisher: Only the Bluebook ends a code citation with the year. Citation is made to the year that appears on the spine of the bound volume, on the title page, or the most recent copyright year (in that order of preference) and the name of the publisher, in parentheses. Note, however that in the rare instances where a code is published under the supervision of federal or state officials, the publisher's name is not required, only the year of publication.

The California Style Manual only identifies the publisher and year when citing editorial materials following annotated code sections (see § 5:2 above).

Parentheses: The California Style Manual only allows abbreviations and symbols when the code citation appears in parentheses. Code citations not integral to the sentence in which they appear are enclosed in parentheses. The Bluebook only encloses the year of decision and the publisher in parentheses.

Commas: Only the California Style Manual uses a comma between the abbreviated title of the code and the section symbol.

"Cal." preface to code titles: Only the Bluebook prefaces code titles with the abbreviation "Cal." California Style Manual format assumes that all codes cited are California codes unless otherwise specified.

Section symbols and spacing: Both manuals include a space between the section symbol and the section reference.

Subdivisions: The California Style Manual requires that the Legislature's exact subdivision designations be used. When citing more than one subdivision, an ampersand (&) or the word "and" is used before the last subdivision cited.

Cross-references: Cal. Style Manual §§ 2:5–2.7. Bluebook, Rules 12.2–12.3.2, pp. 74–78; Table T.1, pp. 173–175.

§ 5:4   Citations to California codes in pocket parts or supplements

General rule: The California Style Manual does not distinguish statutory provisions that appear in supplements or pocket parts from provisions in the main volumes unless citing editorial materials from annotated codes. (For a discussion of citing annotated codes, see § 5:2 above.)

The Bluebook requires citations to supplements or pocket parts, regardless of whether editorial material from the supplement or pocket part is being cited.

California Style Manual:

[None ordinarily required, but see Cal. Style Manual § 2:6]

Bluebook:

Cal. Ins. Code § 501 (Deering Supp. 1998).

Cal. Civ. Proc. Code § 1141.1 (West Supp. 1999).

The year in parentheses refers to the year on the title page of the supplement or pocket part. No distinction is made between pocket parts and supplements; the abbreviation "Supp." applies to both.

When citing both the main volume and the supplement or pocket part, use the following form:

Bluebook:

Cal. Ins. Code § 501 (Deering 1992 & Supp. 1998).

Cal. Civ. Proc. Code § 1141.1 (West 1982 & Supp. 1999).

Cross-references: Cal. Style Manual § 2:9. Bluebook, Rule 3.2(c), p. 34; Rule 12.3.1, pp. 76–77.

§ 5:5   Short forms for code citations

In the California Style Manual, once a code section or rule is cited in full, it is not necessary to repeat the code name or the set of rules in the same paragraph. It is sufficient to merely refer to the section or rule being discussed. However, if referring to a previously cited code section or rule in subsequent paragraphs, use a footnote or parenthetical information to explain that all further references are to the code or a particular set of rules.

The use of "*id.*" in referring to a previous code section or set of rules is appropriate where there is no intervening citation and there is a change from the prior cite. "*Ibid.*" may be used where there are no intervening citations, but where citation is to a different page or section number from the prior cite. The term "*supra*" is never used.

In the Bluebook, short form citations are similar to those prescribed by the California Style Manual, including the use of footnotes to explain subsequent references. However, when using "*id.*," do not use "at" before the section symbol (e.g., "*Id.* § 7," instead of "*Id.* at § 7").

Cross-references: Cal. Style Manual § 2:5. See Bluebook, Rule 12.9, pp. 86–87; Rule 3.4, p. 37; Rule 4.1, p. 40. See also § 1:6 of this guide.

§ 5:6   Order of cited authority

In both manuals, statutory authority precedes case law. For a complete discussion, see § 1:7.

§ 5:7   Citing annotated codes

General rule: In the California Style Manual, annotated codes are only cited when relying on editorial materials such as Law Revision Commission Comments or historical notes following statutory provisions. In practice, such citations ordinarily follow the signal "See," as illustrated below. When both Deering and West publish the editorial materials (such as Law Revision Commission Comments), citations to both editions, separated by a semicolon, should be used.

California Style Manual:

(See Cal. Law Revision Com. coms., Deering's Ann. Civ. Code (1999
   Supp.), § 1141.1, pp. 10–11; West's Ann. Code Civ. Proc. (1999 Supp.)
   § 1141.1, p. 5.)

(See cases collected in Deering's Ann. Code Civ. Proc. (1995 ed.) foll. § 437c under heading Nature, Purpose, and Scope of Proceedings, p. 310.)

(See Suggested Forms, Deering's Ann. Veh. Code, § 26451 (1998 Supp.) p. 332.)

Bluebook:

See Law Revision Com. cmts., Cal. Civ. Proc. Code § 1141.1 (West 1999).

See cases collected in Cal. Civ. Proc. Code (Deering 1995) following § 437c under heading Amendments, p. 310.)

See Suggested Forms, Cal. Veh. Code (Deering Supp. 1998) p. 332.

Cross-references: Cal. Style Manual § 2.9. Bluebook, Table T.1, p. 174.

§ 5:8   Code title abbreviations

General rule: The majority of abbreviations for code titles are identical in both manuals, however, there are some small differences. The primary difference is that the Bluebook includes the word "Cal." before each abbreviated title.

Table 11
Code Title Abbreviations

Code Title	California Style Manual	Bluebook
Business and Professions Code	Bus & Prof. Code	Bus. & Prof. Code[a]
California Uniform Commercial Code	Cal. U. Com. Code	Com. Code
Civil Code	Civ. Code[b]	Civ. Code [b]
Code of Civil Procedure	Code Civ. Proc.[c]	Civ. Proc. Code[c]
Commercial Code	Com. Code	Com. Code
Corporations Code	Corp. Code	Corp. Code
Education Code	Ed.. Code	Educ. Code
Elections Code	Elec. Code	Elec. Code

Table 11—*Continued*

Code Title	California Style Manual	Bluebook
Evidence Code	Evid. Code	Evid. Code
Family Code	Fam. Code	Fam. Code
Financial Code	Fin. Code	Fin. Code
Fish and Game Code	Fish & G. Code	Fish & Game Code
Food and Agricultural Code	Food & Agr. Code	Food & Agric. Code
Government Code	Gov. Code	Gov't. Code
Harbors and Navigation Code	Harb. & Nav. Code	Harb. & Nav. Code
Health and Safety Code	Health & Saf. Code	Health & Safety Code
Insurance Code	Ins. Code	Ins. Code
Labor Code	Lab. Code	Lab. Code
Military and Veterans Code	Mil. & Vet. Code	Mil. & Vet. Code
Penal Code	Pen. Code	Penal Code
Probate Code	Prob. Code	Prob. Code
Public Contract Code	Pub. Contract Code	Pub. Cont. Code
Public Resources Code	Pub. Resources Code	Pub. Res. Code
Public Utilities Code	Pub. Util. Code	Pub. Util. Code
Revenue and Taxation Code	Rev. & Tax. Code	Rev. & Tax. Code
Streets and Highways Code	Sts. & Hy. Code	Sts. & High. Code
Unemployment Insurance Code	Unemp. Ins. Code	Unemp. Ins. Code
Uniform Commercial Code	Cal. U. Com. Code	U.C.C.

Table 11—Continued

Code Title	California Style Manual	Bluebook
Vehicle Code	Veh. Code	Veh. Code
Water Code	Wat. Code	Water Code
Welfare and Institutions Code	Welf. & Inst. Code	Welf. & Inst. Code

[a] The Bluebook requires the abbreviation "Cal." in code titles. However, "Cal." has been omitted in this table so that the differences in the individual abbreviations are more readily seen.

[b] The abbreviation "C.C." is not used in either manual.

[c] The abbreviation "C.C.P." is not used in either manual.

Cross-references: Cal. Style Manual § 2:8. Bluebook, Table T.1, pp. 174–175; Rule 12.3.1(c), p. 76.

Table 12
Abbreviations Frequently Used in Connection with Code Citations

	California Style Manual	Bluebook
and following	et seq.	et seq.
article[s]	art., arts.	art., arts.
chapter[s]	ch., chs.	ch., chs.
clause[s]	cl., cls.	cl., cls.
comment[s]	com., coms.	cmt., cmts.
division[s]	div., divs.	[none indicated]
page[s]	p., pp.	p., pp.
paragraph[s]	¶, ¶¶ or par., pars.	¶, ¶¶ or para., paras.
part[s]	pt., pts.	pt., pts.
section[s]	§, §§ or sec., secs.	§, §§ or sec., secs.
subdivision[s]	subd., subds.	[none indicated]
title[s]	tit., tits.	tit., tits.

Cross-references: Cal. Style Manual § 2:8. Bluebook, Rule 3.4, p. 37; Table T.16, p. 325.

§ 5:9　Municipal codes

General rule: In the California Style Manual, municipal codes are cited analogously to state statutes in terms of the use of abbreviations and parentheses (see § 5:2).

In the Bluebook, municipal codes are cited by listing the political subdivision (e.g., city or county) first, followed by the state abbreviation, the name of the code, the relevant section, and the year of the code in parentheses. The title of the code is set in large and small capital letters.

California Style Manual:

(San Diego Mun. Code, § 33.502.)

Los Angeles Municipal Code sections 101.2 and 101.3 provide . . .

Bluebook:

San Diego, Cal., Municipal Code § 33.502 (1999).

Los Angeles, Cal, Municipal Code §§ 101.2 and 101.3 (1998) provide . . .

Cross-references: Cal. Style Manual § 2:17. Bluebook, Rule 12.8.2, p. 83.

§ 5:10　California Code of Regulations

General rule: In the California Style Manual, the use of abbreviations and parentheses in citing the California Code of Regulations is analogous to citing state statutes. (See § 5:2.) When the citation commences a sentence or otherwise forms an integral part of the sentence, no abbreviations or parentheses are used. Citation sentences use the abbreviation "Cal. Code Regs.," followed by the abbreviation "tit." for title, the title number, and a section symbol followed by the section number.

In the Bluebook, the use of abbreviations and parentheses in citing the California Code of Regulations is likewise analogous to citing state statutes. The abbreviation "Cal. Code Regs." is followed by the abbreviation "tit." for title, the title number, a comma, then the section symbol and section number and year of publication in parentheses.

California Style Manual:

(Cal. Code Regs., tit. 4, § 106.)

In Title 4 of the California Code of Regulations, section 106 provides . . .

Bluebook:

Cal. Code Regs. tit. 4, § 106 (1998).

In Title 4 of the California Code of Regulations, section 106 provides . . .

Cross-references: Cal. Style Manual § 2:16. Bluebook, Table T.1, p. 175.

§ 5:11 California state and local rules

General rule: In the California Style Manual, citing California Rules of Court (Cal. Rules of Court), local appellate court rules (e.g., "Ct. App., First Dist."), and trial court rules (e.g., "Super. Ct. L.A. County, Local Rules") is analogous to citing state statutes in terms of the use of abbreviations and parentheses. (See § 5:2.)

In the Bluebook, abbreviations are freely used in citing rules. Note, however, that the date the rule was promulgated is not required unless citing a rule that has been repealed.

Table 13
Citing Rules of Court, Appellate and Trial Court Rules, and Rules of Professional Conduct

Rules	California Style Manual	Bluebook
California Rules of Court	(Cal. Rules of Court, rule 342(h).)	Cal. Ct. R. 342(h).
	California Rules of Court, rule 342(h) sets forth the format for separate statements accompanying summary judgment motions.	California Rules of Court, rule 342(h) sets forth the format for separate statements accompanying summary judgment motions.

57

Table 13—*Continued*

Rules	California Style Manual	Bluebook
Local appellate court rules	(Ct. App., First Dist., Local Rules, rule 2(a).) (Ct. App. Fourth Dist., Local Rules, rule 6.)	[none specified]
Local trial court rules	(Super. Ct. L.A. County, Local Rules, rule 9(b).) (Super. Ct. San Diego County, Local Rules, rule 11.1.)	[none specified]
Rules of Professional Conduct	(Rules Prof. Conduct, rule 2-104(D)(2)(a).) Rule 6-101 of the Rules of Professional Conduct provides . . .	Cal. Rules of Professional Conduct, Rule 8-101 (1997).[a] Rule 6-101 of the California Rules of Professional Conduct provides . . .

[a] By analogy to the Model Rules of Professional Conduct cited in the Bluebook, Rule 12.8.6, pp. 85–86.

Cross-references: Cal. Style Manual §§ 2:18–2:20, 2:23. Bluebook, Rule 12.8.3, p. 83; Rule 12.8.6, p. 85.

CHAPTER 5
—Notes—

CHAPTER 5
—Notes—

CHAPTER 6

CALIFORNIA LEGISLATIVE HISTORY AND GOVERNMENTAL MATERIALS

§ 6:1   Citations to Senate and Assembly bills—Proposed bills

General rule: In the California Style Manual, the name of the legislative body introducing the proposed bill appears first, followed by the abbreviation "Bill No." and its assigned number, a comma, and then in parentheses, the two-year legislative session in which the bill was introduced (e.g., "1993–1994 Reg. Sess."). During the regular two-year session ("Reg. Sess."), the governor may call a special session to address issues specified in a particular proclamation. In such cases, the sessions are named "1st Extraordinary Session" ("1st Ex. Sess."), "2nd Extraordinary Session" ("2nd Ex. Sess.") and so on. The abbreviation for the session is always preceded by the two-year session in which the extraordinary session is commenced.

If the citation is an independent clause (i.e., the citation can be omitted and the meaning of the sentence is not affected), parentheses are used to enclose the entire citation and the name of the legislative body is abbreviated (e.g., "Sen." or "Assem.").

In the Bluebook, the name of the legislative body introducing the bill (e.g., "Sen." or "Assem.") is abbreviated, followed by the word "Bill" and its assigned number, a comma, the session in which the bill was introduced (e.g., "Reg. Sess." *or* "1st Ex. Sess."), and in parentheses, an abbreviation for the state ("Cal.") and the year.

California Style Manual:

(Assem. Bill No. 6 (1999–2000 1st Ex. Sess.).)

Senate Bill No. 2028 (1997–1998 Reg. Sess.), proposed a revision to . . .

(Sen. Bill No. 1800 (1993–1994 Reg. Sess.).)

Bluebook:

Assem. Bill 6, 1999–2000 1st Ex. Sess. (Cal. 1999).

Assembly Bill 109, 1999–2000 Reg. Sess. (Cal. 1999), provides in pertinent part, . . .

Senate Bill 2028, 1997–1998 Reg. Sess. (Cal. 1999), proposed a revision to . . .

Use of "No.": Unlike the California Style Manual, the Bluebook does not use the abbreviation "No." to preface the bill number.

Parenthetical information: Only the Bluebook requires the abbreviation for the state in which the Legislature sits and the year of publication.

Cross-references: Cal. Style Manual § 2:25[A]. Bluebook, Rule 12.4(b), p. 79; Rule 13.2(c), p. 90; Table T.9, p. 175.

§ 6:2 Citations to Senate and Assembly bills—Enacted bills

General rule: When bills are enacted, they are assigned a chapter number by the Secretary of State and are printed in Statutes and Amendments to the Code (Stats.). In the California Style Manual, the abbreviation "Stats." and the year the bill is enacted appears first, and then between commas, the abbreviation "ch." for chapter and the assigned chapter number, followed by a section symbol, the section number, and a comma, and finally, by the abbreviation "p." and the page number. In the event a bill was enacted in an extraordinary session (e.g., "1st Ex. Sess."), such information is indicated between commas following the year of enactment.

The Bluebook does not distinguish between proposed bills and enacted bills. Although the Bluebook requires that the number of the legislative body be included in the citation, this is not readily ascertainable information in California. Therefore, the examples used below have been modified to fit California session laws and are generally consistent with Bluebook format. The Bluebook recommends that a parallel citation to Statutes and Amendments to the Code be provided; note that the Bluebook uses the abbreviation "Cal. Stat." instead of "Stats."

California Style Manual:

(Stats. 1998, ch. 34, § 1, p. 93.)

(Stats. 1993, ch. 93, § 6, p. 54.)

(Stats. 1997, 1st Ex. Sess. 1996, ch. 456, § 3, p. 1102.)

Bluebook:

Sen. Bill 2028, 1997–1998 Reg. Sess., ch. 34, 1998 Cal. Stat. 1, p. 93.

Sen. Bill 1800, 1993–1994 Reg. Sess., ch. 93, 1994 Cal. Stat. 6, p. 54.

Assem. Bill 1292, 1997–1998 1st Ex. Sess., ch. 456, 1997 Cal. Stat. 3, p. 1102.

Cross-references: Cal. Style Manual § 2:11. Bluebook, Rule 12.4(b), p. 79; Rule 13.2(c), p. 90.

§ 6:3   Citations to Senate and Assembly bills—Citing statutes from advance legislative services

General rule: Recently enacted bills are published by chapter number in West's California Legislative Service or Deering's California Advance Legislative Service at an early date. In the California Style Manual, the abbreviation "Stats." for Statutes and Amendments to the Codes, is followed by the year of enactment and a comma, the chapter number, the number of the volume in which the statute is printed, and the abbreviation of the service, followed by a comma and the relevant page number. Once a bill appears in Statutes and Amendments to the Codes, there is no need to include a parallel citation to a service.

In the Bluebook, when citing bills appearing in a service, the date of enactment and the name of the service is provided in parentheses along with the name of the publisher (also in a set of parentheses). When the bill is printed in Statutes and Amendments to the Codes, a citation to "Cal. Stat." should be given instead of a citation to the service.

California Style Manual:

(Stats. 1998, ch. 34, No. 5 Deering's Adv. Legis. Service, p. 93.)

(Stats. 1993, ch. 93, No. 9 West's Cal. Legis. Service, p. 54.)

(Stats. 1997, ch. 456, No. 3 West's Cal. Legis. Service, p. 1102).

Bluebook:

Sen. Bill 2028, 1997–1998 Reg. Sess. (1998 Cal. Adv. Legis. Serv. (Deering)).

Sen. Bill 1800, 1993–1994 Reg. Sess. (1994 Cal. Legis. Serv. (West)).

Assem. Bill No. 1292, 1997–1998 Reg. Sess. (1998 Cal. Adv. Legis. Serv. (Deering)).

Cross-references: Cal. Style Manual § 2:10. Bluebook, Rule 13.2, p. 90; Table T.1, p. 175.

§ 6:4   Senate and Assembly resolutions

General rule: In the California Style Manual, Senate and Assembly resolutions are cited analogously to bills (as discussed in § 6:1). However, once a resolution is adopted, it is assigned a resolution chapter number and published in Statutes and Amendments to the Codes (Stats.). An adopted resolution is cited by designating the legislative body that introduced it (e.g., "Assem." or "Sen."), an abbreviation for the resolution (either "Res." or "Conc." or "Joint"), the resolution number, and then the following information in parentheses: the abbreviation "Stats.," followed by the session in parentheses (i.e., the two-year session, designating whether it was a regular ("Reg.") or extraordinary ("Ex.") session), and then the abbreviation "res. ch." for resolution chapter, the assigned number, and the relevant page number.

In the Bluebook, resolutions are also cited analogously to bills. Citations to Statutes and Amendments to the Codes are used for adopted resolutions "if it would assist the reader in locating an enacted resolution." An abbreviation for the resolution and its assigned number is followed by the number of the legislative body, the legislative session, and a citation to the Statutes and Amendments to the Code (volume number, the abbreviation "Stats." and the year of enactment). In California, the number of the legislative body is not readily ascertainable. Therefore, the examples below omit this information.

California Style Manual:

(Assem. Conc. Res. No. 82, Stats. (1991–1992 Reg. Sess.) res. ch. 80, p. 7039.)

(Sen. Conc. Res. No. 63, Stats. (1991–1992 Reg. Sess.) res. ch. 5, pp. 6959–6960.)

(Assem. Res. No. 1 (1995–1996 Reg. Sess.).)

(Sen. Joint Res. No. 1, Stats. (1993–1994 Reg. Sess.) res. ch. 6, p. 1039.)

Senate Joint Resolution No. 1, Stats. (1997–1998 Reg. Sess.) res. ch. 12, p. 365, provides . . .

(Assem. Conc. Res. No. 5, Stats. (1997–1998 Reg. Sess.) res. ch. 34, p. 69.)

Assembly Concurrent Resolution No. 40, Stats. (1997–1998 Reg. Sess.) res. ch. 4, p. 5687, contains . . .

House Resolution No. 2 (1997–1998 Reg. Sess.) proposes that . . .

(H. Res. No. 2 (1997–1998 Reg. Sess.).)

Bluebook:

Assem. Conc. Res. 82, 1991–1992 Reg. Sess., 3 Cal. Stat. 7039.

Sen. Res. 63, 1991–1992 Reg. Sess., 3 Cal. Stat. 6959.

Assem Res. 1, 1995–1996 Reg. Sess. (Cal. 1995).

Sen. Joint Res. 1, 1993–1994 Reg. Sess., 12 Cal. Stat. 1039.

Senate Joint Resolution No. 1, 12 Cal. Stat. 1994 (1993–1994 Reg. Sess.) res. ch. ___, pp. ___, provides . . .

Assem. Conc. Res. No. 5, ___ Cal. Stat. (1997–1998 Reg. Sess.) res. ch. ___, pp. ___.

Assembly Concurrent Resolution No. 40, Cal. Stat. (1997–1998 Reg. Sess.) res. ch. ___, pp. ___ contains . . .

House Res. 2, 1997–1998 Reg. Sess., proposes that . . .

H. Res. 2 (1997–1998 Reg. Sess.).

Cross-references: Cal. Style Manual § 2:26; Bluebook, Rule 13.2(c), p. 90.

§ 6:5 Constitutional amendments

General rule: In the California Style Manual, proposed constitutional amendments are cited by the legislative body that introduces them, the assigned amendment number and the session. Once a constitutional amendment is enacted, it is published in Statutes and Amendments to the Code and parallel citations should be used.

The Bluebook does not specifically address proposed constitutional amendments. The examples cited below are consistent with the format prescribed for citing bills and resolutions discussed in § 6:2.

California Style Manual:

(Sen. Const. Amend. No. 1 (1997–1998 Reg. Sess.).)

(Assem. Const. Amend. No. 5 (1999–2000 Reg. Sess.).)

Senate Constitutional Amendment No. 20 (Stats. 1992 (Reg. Sess.) res. ch. 110, pp. 3392–3393) provides . . .

(Assem. Const. Amend. No. 14, Stats. 1992 (1991–1992 Reg. Sess.) res. ch. 6, pp. 6691–6692.)

Bluebook:

Sen. Const. Amend. 1, 1997–1998 Reg. Sess. (Cal. 1998).

Assem. Const. Amend. 1, 1997–1998 Reg. Sess. (Cal. 1998).

Senate Constitutional Amendment 20, Reg. Sess., 110 Cal. Stat. 3392–3393 (Cal. 1992) provides . . .

Assem. Const. Amend. 14, Reg. Sess., 6 Cal. Stat. 6691–6692 (1992).

Cross-references: Cal. Style Manual § 2:27. Cf. Bluebook, Rule 13.2(c), p. 90.

§ 6:6 California legislative committee reports

General rule: In the California Style Manual, the name of the committee appears first, followed by the name of the report, the bill to which it applies, the legislative session, a date identifying the version of the legislation, if material, and a point page. Note that abbreviations are allowed where citations are enclosed in parentheses.

In the Bluebook, the abbreviation for the name of the legislative body appears first, then the number of the report or document, the number of the legislative session and the year of publication in parentheses. Unless it is obvious from the citation, include the abbreviation "Cal." before the year of publication. Where a report has a specific title, the title of the report is given in initial capital letters, followed by an abbreviation for the legislative body and the bill number, the number of the legislative session and the year of publication in parentheses.

California Style Manual:

(Sen. Com. on Judiciary, analysis of Sen. Bill 1237 (1999–2000 Reg. Sess.) passed as amended May 26, 1999.)

(Assem. Com. on Judiciary, recommendation to pass Sen. Bill 1237 (1999–2000 Reg. Sess.) as amended, June 29, 1999.)

(Sen. Com. on Appropriations, fiscal summary of Sen. Bill 1237 (1999–2000 Reg. Sess.) August 30, 1999.)

The Senate Permanent Factfinding Committee, Report on Natural and Geothermal Resources, section 1, page 9, appendix to Senate Journal (1987–1998 Reg. Sess.) explains in great detail the effect . . .

(See Sen. Permanent Factfinding Com., Rep. on Natural and Geothermal Resources, § 1, p. 9, appen. to Sen. J. (1987–1988 Reg. Sess.).)

Bluebook:

S. Comm. on Judiciary, analysis of S. 1237, 1999–2000 Reg. Sess. (passed as amended May 26, 1999).

Assem. Comm. on Judiciary, recommendation to pass S. 1237, 1999–2000 Reg. Sess. (as amended, June 29, 1999).

S. Comm. on Appropriations, fiscal summary of S. 1237, 1999–2000 Reg. Sess. (August 30, 1999).

The Senate Permanent Factfinding Committeee, Report on Natural and Geothermal Resources, § 1, p. 9, app. to S. Journal (1987–1998 Reg. Sess.) explains in great detail the effect . . .

See Sen. Permanent Factfinding Comm., Report on Natural and Geothermal Resources, § 1, p. 9, app. to S.J. (1987–1988 Reg. Sess.).

Cross-references: Cal. Style Manual § 2:28. Bluebook, Rule 13.4(d), pp. 91–92.

§ 6:7   Law Revision Commission reports, comments, studies, and papers

General rule: In the California Style Manual, Law Revision Commission Reports are cited by the full name of the report, the number assigned to it and, in parentheses, the month and year the report is dated, followed by the volume in which the report appears, the abbreviation "Cal. Law Revision Com. Rep." and the year of publication in parentheses and then the page number.

In the Bluebook, no particular mention of Law Revision Commission reports is addressed. Hence the examples used below are in keeping with general Bluebook style and format.

California Style Manual:

(Recommendations Relating to Sovereign Immunity, No. 1, Tort Liability of Public Entities and Public Employees (Jan. 1983), 4 Cal. Law Revision Com. Rep. (1983) p. 817.)

(17 Cal. Law Revision Com. Rep. (Sept. 1993) pp. 711–714.)

In Michael Asimow's Report on the Adjudication Process, reprinted in 25 Cal. Law Revision Com. Rep. (1995) p. 447, Asimow concludes . . .

Bluebook:

Recommendations Relating to Sovereign Immunity, No. 1, Tort Liability of Public Entities and Public Employees (Jan. 1983), 4 Cal. Law Revision Comm. Rep. 817 (1983).

17 Cal. Law Revision Comm. Rep. 711–714 (Sept. 1993).

In Michael Asimow's Report on the Adjudication Process, reprinted in 25 Cal. Law Revision Comm. Rep. 447 (1995), Asimow concludes . . .

Cross-references: Cal. Style Manual § 2:33. For Legislative Counsel reports, opinions, and digests, see Cal. Style Manual § 2:29. For legislative journals, Governor's messages, and executive orders, see Cal. Style Manual § 2:31.

CHAPTER 6
—Notes—

CHAPTER 6
—Notes—

CHAPTER 7

FEDERAL CASES

❖

§ 7:1 United States Supreme Court cases

General rule: In both manuals, United States Supreme Court cases are cited in the same general format as California cases, that is, in the California Style Manual, the citation sentence is ordinarily enclosed in parentheses and the year immediately follows the case name. Whereas, in the Bluebook, the citation sentence is not ordinarily enclosed in parentheses; only the year of decision appears in parentheses at the end of the citation. As discussed below, the two manuals differ slightly in the use of abbreviations and parallel citation requirements.

California Style Manual:

(Thompson v. Keohane, Warden et al. (1995) 516 U.S. 99.)

(Sheet Metal Workers v. EEOC (1985) 478 U.S. 421.)

(Shapiro v. Thompson (1968) 394 U.S. 618.)

Bluebook:

Thompson v. Keohane, Warden et al., 516 U.S. 99 (1995).

Sheet Metal Workers v. EEOC, 478 U.S. 421 (1985).

Shapiro v. Thompson, 394 U.S. 618 (1968).

Cross-references: Cal. Style Manual § 1:32. See generally Bluebook, Table T.1, p. 165.

§ 7:2 Abbreviations for United States Supreme Court reporters

General rule: Both manuals use the same abbreviations for all reporters of the United States Supreme Court except for United States Law Week. However, as with the California reporters, the Bluebook editors like more breathing room and have inserted spaces between some of the abbreviations.

Table 14
Abbreviations for Reporters of United States Supreme Court Decisions

Reporter	California Style Manual	Bluebook
United States Supreme Court Reporter	U.S.	U.S.
Supreme Court Reporter	S.Ct.	S. Ct.

Table 14—*Continued*

Reporter	California Style Manual	Bluebook
Laywer's Edition	L.Ed., L.Ed.2d	L. Ed., L. Ed. 2d
United States Law Week	U.S.L.Week	U.S.L.W.

Cross-references: Cal. Style Manual § 1:32[B]. Bluebook, Rule 10.4(a), p. 63.

§ 7:3 Parallel citations to United States Supreme Court reporters

General rule: The California Style Manual requires parallel citations for the first reference and only the official report citation in subsequent references. The Bluebook does not require parallel citations.

When only unofficial cite available: The California Style Manual still requires use of a parallel citation to the official reports when a case is first referenced, even if the volume and page numbers to the official reporter are unknown. In such cases, the volume and page numbers are indicated by underscoring.

In the Bluebook, if the official cite ("U.S") is unavailable, citations should be to the following reporters: "S. Ct.," "L. Ed.," or "U.S.L.W.," and in that order of preference.

California Style Manual:

(*Saratoga Fishing Co. v. J.M. Martinac & Co.* (1997) ___ U.S. ___ [138 L.Ed.2d 76].)

(*Saratoga Fishing Co. v. J.M. Martinac & Co.* (1997) ___ U.S. ___ [117 S.Ct. 1783].)

(*Saratoga Fishing Co. v. J.M. Martinac & Co.* (1997) ___ U.S. ___ [65 U.S.L.Week 4429, 4431].)

Bluebook:

Saratoga Fishing Co. v. J.M. Martinac & Co., 117 S. Ct. 1783 (1977).

Saratoga Fishing Co. v. J.M. Martinac & Co., 138 L. Ed. 2d 76 (1997).[1]

Saratoga Fishing Co. v. J.M. Martinac & Co., 65 U.S.L.W. 4429 (1977).[2]

---

1 Used only if Supreme Court Reporter citation is unavailable.

2 Used only if Supreme Court Reporter and Lawyer's Edition citations are unavailable.

Cross-references: Cal. Style Manual § 1:32[B]. Bluebook, Table T.1, p. 165.

§ 7:4   Slip opinions of the United States Supreme Court

General rule: Prior to publication in a reporter, recent United States Supreme Court decisions are printed as separate slip opinions identified in both manuals by case name, the date of decision, the docket number, and an indication that it is a United States Supreme Court decision.

Besides the customary differences in sequence and punctuation, the California Style Manual, requires a citation to the official U.S. reporter with the unknown volume and page numbers indicated by underscoring. The Bluebook does not require a "U.S." citation, but does include the abbreviation "U.S." in the parentheses with the date of decision so that the court of decision is clear from the citation.

California Style Manual:

(Ohio Forestry Association, Inc. v. Sierra Club (May 18, 1998) No. 97-16 ___ U.S. ___ .)

Bluebook:

Ohio Forestry Association Inc. v. Sierra Club, No. 97-16 (U.S. May 18, 1998).

Point pages: To cite to a particular page of a slip opinion, use the abbreviation "slip op. at," followed by the point page, or "slip op. 3456, 3458" (which indicates the page on which the opinion starts, and the point page).

Cross-references: Cf. Cal. Style Manual § 1:19. Bluebook, Rule 10.8.1, pp. 68–69.

§ 7:5   United States Supreme Court decisions from electronic databases

General rule: Both manuals permit citations to Westlaw or Lexis databases when decisions are so recent they have yet to be published in a reporter. The rules pertaining to citing United States Supreme Court decisions and all other federal cases are analogous to those pertaining to state court cases discussed in § 1:9.

Cross-references: Cal. Style Manual § 1:3. Bluebook, Rule 10.8.1, pp. 68–69.

§ 7:6 Early United States Supreme Court decisions (1790–1874)

General rule: Decisions of the United States Supreme Court reported from 1790 to 1874 are referred to as early reports and include the reporter editors' names.

In both manuals, the abbreviation of the reporter editor's name appears along with the original volume number in parentheses. In both manuals, this parenthetical information is inserted in the citation following the "U.S." abbreviation for the United States Supreme Court Reports. Aside from the customary differences in the use of parentheses and sequence, the California Style Manual requires a parallel citation when a citation is first referenced (and thereafter a shortened citation to the official report only) while the Bluebook requires no parallel citation.

California Style Manual:

(Marbury v. Madison (1805) 5 U.S. (1 Cranch) 137 [2 L.Ed. 60].)

(Scott v. Sandford (1856) 60 U.S. (19 How.) 393 [15 L.Ed. 691].)

(The Sea Gull (1874) 90 U.S. (23 Wall.) 165 [23 L.Ed. 175].)

Bluebook:

Marbury v. Madison, 5 U.S. (1 Cranch) 137 (1805).

Scott v. Sandford, 60 U.S. (19 How.) 393 (1856).

The Sea Gull, 90 U.S. (23 Wall.) 165 (1874).

Cross-references: Cal. Style Manual § 1:32[D], cf. § 1:3. Bluebook, Table T.1, p. 165.

§ 7:7 United States Court of Appeals decisions

General rule: When citing United States Court of Appeals decisions (reported in West's Federal Reporter and identified by numbered circuits), the California Style Manual requires that the title of the case be in italics, followed by the circuit and year of decision in parentheses, then by the volume number of the official reporter, an abbreviation for the official reporter ("Fed.," "F.2d," or "F.3d") and the page number, followed by a period. The entire citation sentence is enclosed in parentheses regardless of where it appears in the text unless it forms an integral part of the sentence.

The Bluebook cites United States Court of Appeals decisions in identical fashion, except for sequence and punctuation.

The abbreviations for all United States Court of Appeals case reporters are identical in both manuals (including spacing). West's Federal Reporter abbreviations include "F.," "F.2d," and "F.3d." The only difference is that in the California Style Manual, all citations to the first series decisions use the abbreviation "Fed.," not "F."

California Style Manual:

(Beckwith v. Clark (8th Cir. 1911) 188 Fed. 171.)

(McDonald's Corporation v. U.S. (Fed. Cir. 1991) 926 F.2d 1126.)

(Cloverleaf Standardbred Owners v. National Bank (D.C. Cir. 1983) 699 F.2d 1274.)

(In re Grand Jury Proceedings (9th Cir. 1994) 33 F.3d 1060.)

Bluebook:

Beckwith v. Clark, 177 F. 171 (8th Cir. 1911).

McDonald's Corporation v. U.S., 926 F.2d 1126 (Fed. Cir. 1991).

Cloverleaf Standardbred Owners v. National Bank, 699 F.2d 1274 (D.C. Cir. 1983).

In re Grand Jury Proceedings, 33 F.3d 1060 (9th Cir. 1994).

Cross-references: Cal. Style Manual § 1:33. Bluebook, Rule 10.4(a), pp. 63–64; Table T.1, pp. 165–166.

§ 7:8   Cases from other federal appellate courts

General rule: When citing cases from other federal appellate courts (e.g., United States Court of Appeals for the Federal Circuit, the United States Court of Customs and Patents Appeals, or the United States Court of Federal Claims), use the format illustrated in Table 15 below. Aside from the customary differences of sequence and the use of commas and parentheses, on occasion, the manuals use different abbreviations when referring to the various reporters. Both manuals prefer use of the Federal Reporter citation if available.

Table 15
Citations from Other Federal Appellate Courts

Emergency Court of Appeals	California Style Manual	Bluebook
Temporary Emergency Court of Appeals (in existence from 1971–1993)	(*Mobil Oil Corporation v. Dept. of Energy* (T.E.C.A. 1979) 610 F.2d 961.)	*Mobil Oil Corporation*, 610 F.2d 961 (Temp. Emer. Ct. App. 1979).
U.S. Court of Appeals and Court of Customs and Patent Appeals		
U.S. Court of Appeals for the Federal Circuit (created 1982 to succeed U.S. Court of Customs and Patent Appeals and Court of Claims)	(*Stickel v. Heublein, Inc.* (Fed. Cir. 1983) 716 F.2d 1550.)	*Stickel v. Heublein, Inc.* 716 F.2d 1550 (Fed. Cir. 1983).
U.S. Court of Customs and Patent Appeals (1929–1982)	(*B.R. Baker Co. v. Lebow Bros.* (C.C.P.A. 1945) 150 F.2d 580.)	*B.R. Baker Co. v. Lebow Bros.*, 150 F.2d 580 (C.C.P.A. 1945).
Court of Customs Appeals (1910–1929) (predecessor of U.S. Court of Customs and Patent Appeals)	(*Charles L. Barnes v. U.S.* (1910) 46 Ct.Cust. 7.)	*Charles L. Barnes v. U.S.*, 46 Ct. Cust. 7 (1910).
Court of Claims (1956–1982)	(*Brainard Steel Corp. v. U.S.* (Ct.Cl. 1956) 146 F.Supp. 461.)	*Brainard Steel Corp. v. U.S.*, 137 Ct. Cl. 114 (1956).
U.S. Court of Federal Claims		
U.S. Court of Federal Claims (created 1992 to supersede U.S. Claims Court) (West's Federal Claims Reporter)	(*Yankee Atomic Electric Co. v. U.S.* (1995) 33 Fed.Cl. 580.)	*Yankee Atomic Electric Co. v. U.S.*, 33 Fed. Cl. 580 (1995).
U.S. Claims Court (1982–1992)	(*Twin City Shipyard, Inc. v. U.S.* (1991) 23 Cl.Ct. 801.)	*Twin City Shipyard, Inc. v. U.S.*, 23 Cl. Ct. 801 (1991).

Table 15—*Continued*

U.S. Court of Federal Claims	California Style Manual	Bluebook
Court of Claims (1930–1932)	(*Todd v. U.S.* (Ct.Cl. 1931) 46 F.2d 589.)	*Todd v. U.S.*, 46 F.2d 589 (Ct. Cl. 1931).
Court of Claims (1932–1960)	(*American Propeller & Mfg. Co. v. U.S.* (Ct.Cl. 1936) 14 F.Supp. 168.)	*American Propeller & Mfg. Co. v. U.S.*, 14 F.Supp. 168 (Ct. Cl. 1936).
Court of Claims (1960–1982)	(*Mississippi Shipping Co. v. U.S.* (Ct.Cl. 1961) 287 F.2d 910.)	*Mississippi Shipping Co. v. U.S.*, 287 F.2d 910 (Ct. Cl. 1961).
Court of Claims (1863–1982)	(*Tide Water Oil Company v. U.S.* (1896) 31 Ct.Cl. 90.)	*Tide Water Oil Company v. U.S.*, 31 Ct. Cl. 90 (1896).

Cross-references: Cal. Style Manual § 1:33[B]. Bluebook, Table T.1, pp. 165–166.

§ 7:9   Federal district court cases

General rule: The only significant difference between the manuals in citing federal district court cases (reported in the Federal Supplement) is the placement of the parenthetical information containing the abbreviation for the district, the state, and the year of decision. In the California Style Manual, the parenthetical information follows the italicized case name, and the citation ends with the volume number, the abbreviation for the Federal Supplement ("F.Supp." or "F.Supp.2d") and the page number. Ordinarily, parentheses enclose the citation sentence.

In the Bluebook, the parenthetical information ends the citation. Only the information regarding the district, state and year of decision is enclosed in parentheses.

California Style Manual:

(*Fukuda v. Los Angeles County* (C.D.Cal. 1986) 630 F.Supp. 228.)

(*Grasso v. United States Postal Service* (D.Conn. 1977) 438 F.Supp. 1231.)

(National Wildlife Federation et al. v. Clark (D.D.C. 1985) 630 F.Supp. 412.)

(Flue-Cured Tobacco Stabilization Corp. v. U.S. E.P.A. (M.D.N.C. 1998) 4 F.Supp.2d 435.)

(Contreras v. Rice (C.D.Cal. 1998) 5 F.Supp.2d 854.)

Bluebook:

Fukuda v. Los Angeles County, 630 F. Supp. 228 (C.D. Cal. 1986).

Grasso v. United States Postal Service, 438 F. Supp. 1231 (D. Conn. 1977).

National Wildlife Federation et al. v. Clark, 630 F. Supp. 412 (D.D.C. 1985).

Flue-Cured Tobacco Stabilization Corp. v. U.S. E.P.A., 4 F. Supp. 2d 435 (M.D.N.C. 1998).

Contreras v. Rice, 5 F. Supp. 2d 854 (C.D. Cal. 1998).

Abbreviations and spacing: In both manuals, abbreviations for federal district courts are identical. However, in the California Style Manual, a space is only used to separate the state from the year of the decision. In the Bluebook, spaces also appear between the abbreviation for "Federal" and "Supplement" and abbreviations for the district and the state. For a discussion of uniform abbreviations to various states, see § 4:2.

District designations: In both manuals, states with only one district, such as Connecticut, use "D." before the state. For multi-districts, such as California, a geographical prefix such as "C." for "Central," or "S." for Southern, or "N." for Northern, is used before the abbreviation "D." for district. Both manuals use "D.D.C." for the District of Columbia, and "Fed." for the Federal District.

Cross-references: Cal. Style Manual § 1:34[A]. Bluebook, Rule 10.4, pp. 63–64.

§ 7:10 Other federal cases published in the Federal Supplement

Aside from publishing United States District Court decisions, the Federal Supplement also publishes decisions of the following courts:

Special Court, Regional Rail Reorganization Act

United States Court of International Trade

Judicial Panel on Multidistrict Litigation

United States Customs Court (until 1980)

Examples of case citations from each court are set forth below. Note the differences in abbreviations, spacing, and sequence.

Special Court, Regional Rail Reorganization Act decisions

California Style Manual:

(*Consolidated Rail Corp. v. Illinois* (Regional Rail Reorg. Ct. 1976) 423 F.Supp. 941.)

Bluebook:

Consolidated Rail Corp. v. Illinois, 423 F. Supp. 941 (Regional Rail Reorg. Ct. 1976).

Cross-references: Cal. Style Manual § 1:34[A]. Bluebook, Table T.1, p. 167.

United States Court of International Trade decisions

California Style Manual:

(*Comitex Knitters, Ltd. v. U.S.* (Ct.Internat.Trade 1992) 803 F.Supp. 411.)

Bluebook:

Comitex Knitters, Ltd. v. U.S., 16 Ct. Int'l Trade 817 (1992).

Comitex Knitters, Ltd. v. U.S., 803 F. Supp. 411 (Ct. Int'l Trade 1992).

Cross-references: Cal. Style Manual § 1:34[A]. Bluebook, Table T.1, p. 166.

Judicial Panel on Multidistrict Litigation decisions

California Style Manual:

(*In re Air Disaster at Lockerbie, Scotland* (J.P.M.L. 1989) 709 F.Supp. 231.)

Bluebook:

In re Air Disaster at Lockerbie, Scotland, 709 F. Supp. 231 (J.P.M.L. 1989).

Cross-references: Cal. Style Manual § 1:34[A]. Bluebook, Rule 10.3.2(a), p. 64; Table T.1, p. 167.

United States Customs Court

California Style Manual:

(*Inter-Maritime Forwarding Co., Inc. v. United States* (Cust.Ct. 1970) 318 F.Supp. 218.)

Bluebook:

Inter-Maritime Forwarding Co., Inc. v. United States, 318 F. Supp. 218 (Cust. Ct. 1970).

Cross-references: Cal. Style Manual § 1:34[A]. Bluebook, Table T.1, p. 166.

§ 7:11 Decisions of the United States bankruptcy courts—General rule

In the California Style Manual, the title of the decision is underscored or italicized, followed by the abbreviation "Bankr.," the circuit and the year of the bankruptcy decision in parentheses, and then a citation to the Bankruptcy Reporter (B.R).

In the Bluebook, the title of the case is either underscored or in italics, followed by the citation to the Bankruptcy Reporter (B.R), and then, in parentheses, the abbreviation "Bankr.," the abbreviation for the district in which the deciding court is located, and the full date of decision. If the case was decided before 1979, it preexists the creation of the Bankruptcy Reporter, therefore, citations to services (e.g., Bankr. L. Rep. (CCH)) should be used instead of the "B.R." citations.

§ 7:12 Decisions of the United States bankruptcy courts—Bankruptcy Court decisions

California Style Manual:

(*In re Rogers* (Bankr. S.D.Cal. 1998) 222 B.R. 348.)

(*In re Stinson* (Bankr. E.D.Mich 1998) 221 B.R. 726.)

(*In re Taylor v. Wood et al.* (Bankr. D.R.I. 1984) Bankr.L.Rep. (CCH) ¶ 64,384 (1972).)

(*Federal's Inc. v. Edmonton Investment Company* (Bankr. S.D.Cal. 1954) Bankr.L.Rep. (CCH) ¶ 66,386 (1997).)

Bluebook:

In re Rogers, 222 B.R. 348 (Bankr. S.D. Cal. June 18, 1998).

In re Stinson, 221 B.R. 726 (Bankr. E.D. Mich. May 29, 1998).

In re Taylor v. Wood et al., Bankr. L. Rep. (CCH) ¶ 64,384 (Bankr. D.R.I. Sept. 8, 1984).

Federal's Inc. v. Edmonton Investment Company, Bankr. L. Rep. (CCH) ¶ 66,386 (Bankr. S.D. Cal. Nov. 18, 1954).

Cross-references: Cal. Style Manual § 1:33[D]. Bluebook, Rule 10.3.1, p. 62; Rule 18.1, p. 129.

§ 7:13 Decisions of the United States bankruptcy courts—Bankruptcy appellate panel decisions

The Bluebook is the only manual that addresses citing decisions of the United States bankruptcy appellate panels. The California Style Manual examples used below are consistent with its general format.

California Style Manual:

(*In re Superior Fast Freight, Inc.* (B.A.P. 9th Cir. 1996) 202 B.R. 485.)

(*In re Merrifield* (B.A.P. 8th Cir. 1997) 214 B.R. 362.)

Bluebook:

In re Superior Fast Freight, Inc., 202 B.R. 485 (B.A.P. 9th Cir. Oct. 5, 1996).

In re Merrifield, 214 B.R. 362 (B.A.P. 8th Cir. Nov. 21, 1997).

Cross-references: Bluebook, Rule 10.4, p. 64; Rule 18.1, p. 129; Table T.1, p. 167.

§ 7:14 Federal cases from advance sheets or advance pamphlet publications

General rule: The California Style Manual cites a decision published in an advance sheet or pamphlet as follows: the title of the case is in italics followed by the applicable circuit court or the district court abbreviation and the full date of the decision in parentheses, an "F.Supp.2d" or "F.3d" citation with unknown volume and page numbers indicated by underscoring, and the full docket number in parentheses. As is customary, unless it is an integral part of a sentence, citations to advance sheets or publications should be enclosed in parentheses.

In the Bluebook, only the full docket number, the district court abbreviation and the full date of the most recent disposition of the case in parentheses is required. Citations to the source in which the federal case will ultimately be reported are not used.

California Style Manual:

(American States Ins. Co. v. Creative Walking, Inc. (E.D.Mo. August 17, 1998) ___ F.Supp.2d ___ [Dock. No. 4:97 CV 1125 SNL].)

(Kaplan v. Cal. Public Employees Retirement Systems (N.D.Cal. Sept. 3, 1998) ___ F.Supp.2d ___ [Dock. No. C 98-1246].)

(U.S. v. Bulacan (9th Cir. Sept. 17, 1998) ___ F.3d ___ [Dock. No. 97-10222].)

(Mas-Hamilton Group v. LaGard, Inc. (Fed.Cir. Sept. 20, 1998) ___ F.3d ___ [Dock. No. 97-1530, 97-1546].)

Bluebook:

American States Ins. Co. v. Creative Walking, Inc., No. 4:97 CV 1125 SNL (E.D. Mo. August 17, 1998).

Kaplan v. Cal. Public Employees Retirement Systems, No. C 98-1246 (N.D. Cal. Sept. 3, 1998).

U.S. v. Bulacan, No. 97-10222 (9th Cir. Sept. 17, 1998).

Mas-Hamilton Group v. LaGard, Inc., No. 97-1530, 97-1546 (Fed. Cir. Sept. 20, 1998).

Cross-references: Cal. Style Manual § 1:34[A]. Bluebook, Rule 10.8.1(b), p. 68.

§ 7:15 Federal cases from computer databases

General rule: Both the California Style Manual and the Bluebook permit citing to a computer database when a federal case has yet to be published in the Federal Reporter or the Federal Supplement.

In the California Style Manual, the title of the case is in italics, followed by the abbreviation for the circuit or district court, the date of filing, and the docket number all enclosed in parentheses, the "F.3d" or

"F.Supp.2d" citation (with underscoring for the unknown volume and page numbers), and finally, the Westlaw or Lexis citation in brackets.

In the Bluebook, the title of the case is either in italics or underscored, followed by a comma and the docket number, a comma and the Westlaw or Lexis citation (including the page or screen number preceded by an asterisk) and then, in parentheses, the abbreviation for the circuit or district court and the full date of the most recent major disposition of the case.

California Style Manual:

(*Accuscan Inc. v. Xerox Corp.* (S.D.N.Y., Sept. 11, 1998, No. 96 Civ. 2579 (HB)) ___ F.Supp.2d ___ [1998 WL 603217].)

(*U.S. v. Bois D'Arc Operating Co.* (E.D.La., Sept. 16, 1998, No. Civ.A. 98-0157) ___ F.Supp.2d ___ [1998 WL 603217].)

(*U.S. v. Bulacan* (9th Cir., Sept. 17, 1998, No. 97-10222) ___ F.3d ___ [1988 WL 635466].)

(*In re Been* (9th Cir., Aug. 31, 1998, No. 97-55486) ___ F.Supp.2d ___ [1998 WL 547122].)

Bluebook:

Accuscan Inc. v. Xerox Corp., No. 96 Civ 2579 (HB), 1998 WL 603217, at *3 (S.D. N.Y. Sept. 11, 1998).

U.S. v. Bois D'Arc Operating Co., No. CIV.A.98-0157, 1998 WL 603217, at *5 (E.D. La. Sept. 16, 1998).

U.S. v. Bulacan, No. 97-10222, 1998 WL 635466, at *10 (9th Cir. Sept. 17, 1998).

In re Been, No. 97-55486, 1998 WL 547122, at *2 (9th Cir. Aug. 31, 1998).

Cross-references: Cal. Style Manual § 1:34, and see § 1:3. Bluebook, Rule 10.8.1(a), p. 68.

§ 7:16 Federal administrative agency decisions and executive materials— National Labor Relations Board decisions

California Style Manual:

(*Wagon Wheel Bowl, Inc., et al.* (1996) 322 NLRB 84.)

Bluebook:

Wagon Wheel Bowl, Inc., et al., 322 N.L.R.B. 84 (1996).

Advance sheet opinions: In the California Style Manual, the case name is in italics followed by the filing date in parentheses and the board-assigned number. In the Bluebook, the case name is either italicized or underscored, followed by the board assigned number and then the filing date in parentheses.

California Style Manual:

(Douglas-Randall, Inc. (Dec. 22, 1995) 320 NLRB No. 14.)

Bluebook:

Douglas-Randall, Inc., 320 N.L.R.B. No. 14 (Dec. 22, 1995).

Cross-references: Cal. Style Manual § 1:35. See generally Bluebook, Rule 13.6, p. 92; Rule 14.3.2(b), p. 96.

§ 7:17 Federal administrative agency decisions and executive materials—Labor Relations Reference Manual

California Style Manual:

(Lehnert v. Ferris Faculty Assn. (1991) 500 U.S. 507 [137 LRRM (BNA) 2321].)

Bluebook:

Lehnert v. Ferris Faculty Assn, 137 L.R.R.M. (BNA) 2321 (1991).

Cross-references: Cal. Style Manual § 1:35[B]. Bluebook, Table T.15, p. 322.

§ 7:18 Federal administrative agency decisions and executive materials—Other cases or decisions

For other federal cases, decisions, and U.S. official administrative publications (such as the Federal Trade Commission Reports), refer to the Bluebook, Rule 14, pp. 93–101 and adapt the citation to the customary format of the California Style Manual.

CHAPTER 7
—Notes—

CHAPTER 8

UNITED STATES CONSTITUTION; FEDERAL STATUTES, RULES, AND OTHER MATERIALS

§ 8:1   United States Constitution

In the California Style Manual, the abbreviation "U.S. Const." appears first, followed by the abbreviation "art." and the article number in roman numerals or the abbreviation "Amend." and the amendment number in arabic numerals, a comma, the section symbol (§) and number, a comma, and if appropriate, the abbreviation "cl." and the number of the clause being referenced. When a citation forms an integral part of a sentence, parentheses are not required, and abbreviations are not allowed. If it is evident from the text that the reference applies to the United States Constitution, it is not necessary to include the words "federal" or "U.S." before the word "Constitution."

In the Bluebook, the abbreviations "U.S. Const.," "amend.," "art.," and "cl." are also used. There is no comma between the abbreviation "Const." and "art." or "Const." and "amend." Arabic numerals are used to reference a particular article, section, or clause. Roman numerals are used to reference a specific amendment.

California Style Manual:

(U.S. Const., art. I, § 6, cl. 1.)

Article I, section 6, clause 1 of the United States Constitution provides U.S. senators and representatives with immunity from arrest for any speech or debate that occurs in either House.

(U.S. Const., 18th Amend., repealed by U.S. Const. 21st Amend.).

Bluebook:

U.S. Const. art. I, § 6, cl. 1.

Article I, § 6, cl. 1 of the U.S. Const. provides U.S. senators and representatives with immunity from arrest for any speech or debate that occurs in either House.

U.S. Const. amend. XVIII, *repealed by* U.S. Const. amend XXI..

Cross-references: Cal. Style Manual § 2:2. Bluebook, Rule 11, p. 73.

§ 8:2 United States Code

General rule: In the California Style Manual, the title number appears first, followed by the abbreviation for the federal code and then the section symbol and number. Cite to the United States Code (U.S.C.) whenever possible since this is the official reporter. The United States Code Annotated (U.S.C.A.) and the United States Code Service (U.S.C.S.) are unofficial reporters. Ordinarily, the year of enactment is not included. If, however, a code provision has been superseded, add the year of enactment in parentheses at the end of the citation. As is customary, citations to federal codes are enclosed in parentheses unless they form an integral part of the sentence. No abbreviations are allowed if the citation is not enclosed in parentheses.

In the Bluebook, the title number appears first followed by the abbreviation for the federal code, the section symbol and number, and, in parentheses, the year of publication. Cite to "U.S.C.," the official reporter, whenever possible. When citing "U.S.C.A." or "U.S.C.S.," insert the name of the publisher (e.g., West) in the parenthetical information before the year of publication. If a code appears in a supplement, include the abbreviation "Supp." in the parenthetical information.

California Style Manual:

(14 U.S.C. § 193.)

(11 U.S.C.A. § 522.)

(46 U.S.C. appen. § 951 (repealed 11/23/98).)

(18 U.S.C.S. § 3182.)

The Ship Mortgage Act (46 U.S.C. § 911 (1920)) is now contained in
Revised Title 46 U.S.C. §§ 31321 to 31330.

Bluebook:

14 U.S.C. § 193 (1995).

11 U.S.C.A. § 522 (West 1990).

46 U.S.C. app. § 951 (*repealed* 11/23/98).

18 U.S.C.S. § 3182 (Law. Co-op. 1989 & Supp. 1993).

The Ship Mortgage Act, 46 U.S.C. § 911 (1920), is now contained in
Revised Title 46 U.S.C. §§ 31321 to 31330 (West Supp. 1998).

Code title abbreviations: Code title abbreviations (including spacing) are identical in both manuals.

Year: The Bluebook requires the year of publication for all citations to federal codes.

Publisher: The Bluebook requires the name of the publisher, in addition to the year of publication, for all citations to the United States Code Annotated or the United States Code Service.

No italics or underscoring: Citations to statutory material are neither italicized nor underscored in either manual.

Identifying supplements or pocket parts: Only the Bluebook requires an author to identify statutes appearing in supplements or pocket parts. The California Style Manual only requires citations to a supplement or pocket part when citing editorial materials from annotated codes. See § 5:4.

Appended material: Both the California Style Manual and the Bluebook require reference to material appearing in an appendix. The only difference between the two manuals is in the abbreviations (i.e., the California Style Manual uses "appen." whereas the Bluebook uses "app.").

Cross-references: Cal. Style Manual § 2:37. Bluebook, Rules 12.3, 12.3.1(b), 12.3.2, pp. 76–78; Table T.1, p. 168.

§ 8:3 Internal Revenue Code

General rule: The current Internal Revenue Code is contained in title 26 of the United States Code. Both manuals allow an author to cite to either the Internal Revenue Code or to "26 U.S.C."

In the California Style Manual, the abbreviation "Int.Rev. Code" appears first, followed by a comma, a section symbol (§), and the section number.

In the Bluebook, the volume and title is followed by the abbreviation "U.S.C." and the section symbol and number, or the abbreviation "I.R.C." and the section symbol and number.

California Style Manual:

(Int.Rev. Code, § 217.)

(26 U.S.C. § 217.)

Section 1117(e) of the Internal Revenue Code of 1939 was the predecessor to section 7459(e).

(Int.Rev. Code, § 894(b)(1) (1939).)

Bluebook:

I.R.C. § 217.

26 U.S.C. § 217.

Section 1117(e) of the I.R.C. (1939) was the predecessor to § 7459(e).

I.R.C. § 894(b)(1) (1939).

Parallel citations: The California Style Manual requires parallel citations when citing a superseded or repealed statute. In such a case, a parallel citation to the Statutes at Large should be used.

Year of enactment: Neither manual requires the year of enactment unless referring to a superseded or repealed statute. In the absence of a year, the assumption under both manuals is that the current version is being cited.

Cross-references: Cal. Style Manual § 2:40. Bluebook, Practitioners' Notes, P.5, pp. 16–17; and Rule 12.8.1, pp. 82–83. For Treasury Regulations and determinations, refer to Bluebook, Rules 14.5.1 and 14.5.2, pp. 97–99.

§ 8:4   Public Laws and Statutes at Large

General rule: In the California Style Manual, slip laws are cited by their official or popular name, the abbreviation "Pub.L. No." for Public Law number, followed by the number of the legislative body (e.g., "94th Congress"), a hyphen, the number assigned to the law, the full date of enactment in parentheses, and the volume and page number of the reporting sources. Use "Act of" plus the year of enactment for cases without a name. Parallel citations to the official reporter, Statutes at Large ("Stat."), are required even if the bound volume has yet to be published. Citations to the United States Code Congressional and Administrative News ("U.S. Code Cong. & Admin. News"), an unofficial source that publishes slip laws at an early date, is also encouraged.

In the Bluebook, slip laws are cited by their official or popular name (or both), the abbreviation "Pub. L. No." for public law number, followed by the number of the legislative body, a hyphen and the number assigned to the law, followed by a citation to the Statutes at Large ("Stat."), and then the year of enactment in parentheses. If the year of enactment is not identified, provide the year the statute became effective. If a statute is so current that it is not cited in the current official code or supplement, then citations should be to the United States Code Congressional and Administrative News ("U.S.C.C.A.N."), computer databases, a looseleaf service, a periodical, or a newspaper, in that order of preference.

California Style Manual:

(Age Discrimination in Employment Act of 1967, Pub.L. No. 90-202 (Dec. 15, 1967), 81 Stat. 602, 1967 U.S. Code Cong. & Admin. News, No. 1, p. 659.)

(Federal Employees Life Insurance Act, Pub.L. No. 105-311 (Oct. 30, 1998), 112 Stat. 2950 (1998), 1998 U.S. Code Cong. & Admin. News, No.11A.)

(Deceptive Mail Prevention and Enforcement Act of 1999, Pub.L. No. 106-168 (Dec. 12, 1999), ___ Stat. ___, U.S. Code Cong. & Admin. News, No. 12D.)

Bluebook:

Age Discrimination in Employment Act of 1967, Pub. L. No. 90-202, 81 Stat. 602 (1967).

Federal Employees Life Insurance Act, Pub. L. No. 105-311, 112 Stat. 2950 (1998).

Deceptive Mail Prevention and Enforcement Act of 1999, Pub. L. No. 106-168, ___ Stat. ___, U.S.C.C.A.N. No. 12D (1999).

Abbreviations: The Bluebook abbreviates the United States Code Congressional and Administrative News by the first letter of each word in the publication's title. In contrast, the California Style Manual simply shortens the words in the title.

Sequence: The sequence of citing a public statute is the same in both manuals; that is, cite to the public law number first, then to the Statutes at Large (if available), and finally to a secondary source, such as the United States Code Congressional and Administrative News or a widely used electronic database.

Sections and point pages: If citing only part of an act, the Bluebook requires the author to provide the sections or subsections cited, as well as the pages on which the cited sections or subsections appear. When citing to an entire act, only the page on which the act begins is required.

Cross-references: Cal. Style Manual §§ 2:38–2:48. Bluebook, Rule 12.1, pp. 73–74; Rule 12.4, pp. 78–80; and Rule 14.9, p. 100.

§ 8:5 Code of Federal Regulations

The California Style Manual cites federal administrative rules and regulations published in the Code of Federal Regulations by title, the volume number, the abbreviation "C.F.R." and the relevant part, section, or page number, followed by the year in parentheses. If the rules and regulations have yet to be printed in the C.F.R., then cite to the Federal Register ("Fed.Reg."), a daily supplement, which prints the rules and regulations at an early date. Citations to the Federal Register should also be to title, section, or part, the abbreviation "Fed.Reg." followed by the page number and the full date of enactment in parentheses. As is customary, the entire citation is enclosed in parentheses unless it forms an integral part of the sentence.

In the Bluebook, citations to the Code of Federal Regulations are to the title, the volume number, the abbreviation "C.F.R.," the section, part, or page, and the year in parentheses. Citations to the Federal Register are to the popular name of the rule or regulation, the volume number, the abbreviation "Fed. Reg.," the page on which the rule or regulation begins, and the complete date of enactment in parentheses. When referring to a particular part or section of a rule or regulation, provide the page number on which the regulation begins, and the page number of the material being cited. If the Federal Register identifies the volume and part, section, or page number in the Code of Federal Regulations where the regulation will ultimately appear, provide that information in parentheses.

California Style Manual:

(Shipping, 46 C.F.R. § 221.1 (1998).)

(Aeronautics and Space, 14 C.F.R. § 13.101 (1997).)

(Health and Human Services, 64 Fed.Reg. 63518-01 (November 19, 1999), [1999 WL 1043469].).

Bluebook:

Shipping, 46 C.F.R. § 221.1 (1998).

Aeronautics and Space, 14 C.F.R. § 13.101 (1997).

Health and Human Services, 64 Fed. Reg. 63518-01 (November 19, 1999), 1999 WL 1043469, at *1.

Abbreviations and spacing: The abbreviations for the Code of Federal Regulations and the Federal Register are identical in both manuals. However, the Bluebook uses a space in "Fed. Reg."

Full date versus year: The California Style Manual requires the full date of enactment for material citing in the Federal Register, whereas the Bluebook only requires the year.

Italics: Note that neither manual italicizes the abbreviation for the Code of Federal Regulations or Federal Register.

Cross-references: Cal. Style Manual § 2:44. Bluebook, Rule 14.2(a), pp. 94–95.

§ 8:6 Federal court rules

In the California Style Manual, federal rules of evidence or procedure are cited similarly to the United States Code (see § 8:4). The title of the rule is abbreviated, followed by a comma, the word "rule," the applicable rule number, another comma, and then the parallel citation to the applicable title number of the United States Code. (See Table 16 below for the abbreviations.) Unless they form an integral part of a sentence, citations to federal court rules are enclosed in parentheses.

Note that in the California Style Manual, the word "rule" is never abbreviated and is only capitalized when it appears in the title of the code (never when referring to a particular rule).

In the Bluebook, the abbreviations to the federal rules of evidence or procedure are set in initial capital letters. No parallel citations are required.

California Style Manual:

(Fed. Rules Civ.Proc., rule 4, 28 U.S.C.)

(Rule 9(b), Fed. Rules App.Proc., as amended October 1, 1992 (28 U.S.C.).)

(U.S. Cir. Ct. Rules (9th Cir.), rule 3-2.)

Rule 4 of the Federal Rules of Civil Procedure (28 U.S.C.) prescribes the appropriate manner for completing service.

Bluebook:

Fed. R. Civ. P. 4.

Rule 9(b), Fed. R. App. P., as amended October 1, 1992.

9th Cir. R. 3-2.

Rule 4 of the Fed. R. Civ. P. prescribes the appropriate manner for completing service.

Cross-references: Cal. Style Manual § 2:46. Bluebook, Rule 12.8.1, p. 83.

Table 16
Abbreviations for Federal Rules of Evidence and Procedure

Rule	California Style Manual	Bluebook
Federal Rules of Civil Procedure, rule 12.	Fed. Rules Civ.Proc., rule 12.	Fed R. Civ. P. 12.
Federal Rules of Criminal Procedure, rule 9.	Fed. Rules Crim.Proc., rule 9.	Fed. R. Crim. P. 9.
Federal Rules of Appellate Procedure, rule 7.	Fed. Rules App.Proc., rule 4.	Fed. R. App. P. 4.

Table 16—*Continued*

Rule	California Style Manual	Bluebook
United States Circuit Court Rules for the 9th Circuit, rule 3.	U.S. Cir. Ct. Rules (9th Cir.), rule 3.	9th Cir. R. 3.
Federal Rules of Evidence, rule 402	Fed. Rules Evid., rule 402.	Fed. R. Evid. 402.
United States Supreme Court Rules, rule 10.	U.S. Supreme Ct. Rules, rule 10.	Sup. Ct. R. 10.

§ 8:7   Congressional bills and resolutions—Unenacted

In the California Style Manual, bills and resolutions generated by Congress are cited by abbreviating the name of the house introducing the material (see Table 17 in § 8:8 for a complete list of abbreviations), the abbreviation "No." and the number assigned to the material, the number of the Congress and the abbreviation (e.g., "105th Cong."), a comma, the number of the session, and the year of publication in parentheses. If the citation does not form an integral part of the sentence, it is enclosed in parentheses regardless of where it falls in the sentence.

In the Bluebook, the name of the house introducing the material is abbreviated, followed by the Congress, the number of the bill or resolution, and the year of publication in parentheses. Since the session number (first or second) can be inferred from the year of publication, none is required (i.e., first sessions fall in odd-numbered years and second sessions fall in even-numbered years). In the unusual event Congress holds a third session, provide the session information in parentheses.

California Style Manual:

(H.R. No. 11764, 105th Cong., 1st Sess., § 1 (1997).)

(Sen. No. 1126, 104th Cong., 2d Sess., § 2 (1996).)

(§ 6(a) of Sen.Res. No. 44, § 7 of H.R. No. 7155, 86th Cong., 1st Sess. (1959).)

Bluebook:

H.R. 11764, 105th Cong. § 1 (1997).

S. 1126, 104th Cong. § 2 (1996).

Section 6(a) of S. Res. 44, H.R. 7155, 86th Cong. § 7 (1959).

Cross-references: Cal. Style Manual § 2:41. Bluebook, Rules 13.1 and 13.2, pp. 88–90.

§ 8:8   Congressional bills and resolutions—Enacted

Once enacted, bills and resolutions become statutes and are reported in the Statutes at Large or the Congressional Record. Accordingly, in both manuals, house resolutions that have been adopted also contain a parallel cite to the Congressional Record or the Statutes at Large. In the Bluebook, unless it is clear from the context or citation that a simple or concurrent resolution has been enacted, the fact of enactment should be noted in parentheses following the year of enactment

California Style Manual:

(Sen.Res. No. 21, 105th Cong., 2d Sess. (1996).).

(Sen.Res. No. 10, 100th Cong., 1st Sess. (1991) 100 Cong. Rec. 100.)

(H.Con.Res. No. 10, 100th Cong., 2d Sess. (1991) 150 Stat. 150.)

Bluebook:

S. Res. 21, 105th Cong. (1996) (enacted).

S. Res. 10, 100th Cong., 100 Cong. Rec. 100 (1991).

H.R. Con. Res. 10, 100th Cong., 150 Stat. 150 (1991).

Cross-references: Cal. Style Manual § 2:41. Bluebook, Rules 13.1, 13.2, pp. 88–90.

Table 17
Abbreviations Used in Citing Bills and Resolutions

Bill or Resolution	California Style Manual	Bluebook
House Bill No. 23	H.R. No. 23	H.R. 23
Senate Bill No. 32	Sen. No. 28	S. 28
House Resolution No. 2	H.Res. No. 2	H.R. Res. 2
House Concurrent Resolution No. 122	H.Con.Res. No. 122	H.R. Con. Res. 122

Table 16—*Continued*

Bill or Resolution	California Style Manual	Bluebook
Senate Resolution No. 39	Sen.Res. No. 39	S. Res.
Senate Concurrent Resolution No. 17	Sen.Con.Res. No. 17	S. Con. Res. 17
House Joint Resolution No. 1	H.J.Res. No. 1	H.R.J. Res. 1
Senate Joint Resolution No. 12	Sen.J.Res. No. 12	S.J. Res. 12

Cross-references: Cal. Style Manual § 2:41[C]. Bluebook, Rules 13, 13.1, 13.2, pp. 88–89. To cite congressional reports, documents, hearings, debates, and addresses, refer to Cal. Style Manual § 2:42; Bluebook, Rules 13.3–13.5. To cite treaties and international agreements, refer to Cal. Style Manual § 2:43; Bluebook, Rule 20.4.5, pp. 142–143.

CHAPTER 8
—Notes—

CHAPTER 9

WITKIN AND OTHER TREATISES, CALIFORNIA PRACTICE GUIDES, SECONDARY SOURCES, AND JURY INSTRUCTIONS

§ 9:1   Witkin and other treatises

General rule: In the California Style Manual, the volume number of the treatise is followed by the author's last name, a comma, the title of the treatise, and in parentheses, the edition and year of publication, then the title of the chapter (optional), a comma, and the section and page number references separated by commas. When two authors collaborate to write a treatise, both last names are included and connected with the word "and," or if the citation is in parentheses, with an ampersand (&). If the treatise is written by more than two authors, only the last name of the first author is used followed by a comma and the abbreviation "et al." As is customary, the citation is enclosed in parentheses unless it forms an integral part of a sentence. Within parentheses, the only abbreviations allowed are "Cal." for "California" and an ampersand for "and."

In the Bluebook, the volume number (if any) is followed by the author's full name, a comma, the title of the treatise in italics or underscored, the section or page number references separated by commas, and the edition number and year of publication in parentheses. No comma appears before a section or a page reference. Titles to treatises may be underscored in court documents, but italics are reserved for chapter titles or articles within larger works.

Witkin examples

California Style Manual:

(6 Witkin, Cal. Procedure (4th ed. 1997) Procedure Without Trial, § 90, p. 491.)

(2 Witkin & Epstein, Cal. Criminal Law (2d ed. 1988) Crimes Against Governmental Authority, § 1141, p. 1322.)

(1 Witkin, Cal. Evidence (3d ed. 1986) Evidence in Non-Jury Trial, § 30, p. 32.)

(1 Witkin, Summary of Cal. Law (9th ed. 1987) Contracts, § 632, p. 569.)

For a comprehensive summary on the law pertaining to crimes against governmental authority, refer to 2 Witkin & Epstein, California Criminal Law (2d ed. 1998), section 1141, page 1322.

Bluebook:

6 Bernard E. Witkin, *California Procedure* § 90, p. 491 (4th ed. 1997).

2 Bernard E. Witkin & Norman L. Epstein, *California Criminal Law* § 1141, p. 1322 (2d ed. 1988).

1 Bernard E. Witkin, *Cal. Evidence* § 30, p. 32 (3d ed. 1986).

1 Bernard E. Witkin, *Summary of California Law* § 632, p. 569 (9th ed. 1987–1990).

For a comprehensive summary on the law pertaining to crimes against governmental authority, refer to 2 Bernard E. Witkin & Norman L. Epstein, *California Criminal Law* § 1141, p. 1322 (2d ed. 1998).

Examples of other popular treatises

California Style Manual:

(24 Couch on Insurance (3d ed. 1999) Specific Property as within Exclusion, § 1:26:24.)

(1 Ballantine & Sterling, Cal. Corporation Laws (4th ed. 1998) Contemporaneous Ownership Requirement, § 292.02[1][a].)

(1 Herlick, Cal. Workers' Compensation Law (5th ed. 1994) Employer Immunity, § 1.2, p. 12-25.)

(5 Miller & Starr, Current Law of Cal. Real Estate (2d ed. 1989) Escrows, § 5:24, p. 342.)

(1 Williston on Contracts (Lord ed. 1990) Unilateral Promise, § 5:13, p. 687.)

Bluebook:

24 George J. Couch & Ronald A. Anderson et al., *Couch on Insurance* § 1:26:24 (3d ed. 1999).

1 Henry Winthrop Ballantine & Graham Lee Sterling, *California Corporation Laws* § 292.02[1][a] (4th ed. 1998).

1 Stanford D. Herlick, *California Workers' Compensation Law* § 1.2, p. 12-25 (5th ed. 1994).

5 Harry D. Miller & Marvin B. Starr, *Current Law of California Real Estate* § 5:24, p. 342 (2d ed. 1989).

4 Samuel Williston & Walter H. E. Jaeger, *A Treatise on the Law of Contracts* § 6:9, p. 245 (4th ed. 1995).

Chapter titles: Recommended but not required by the California Style Manual. Neither recommended nor required by the Bluebook.

Italics or underscored: The Bluebook requires underscoring or italics for the titles of books. Names of authors appear in roman typeface.

Full name of author: Only the Bluebook requires the full name of the author when the treatise is first cited.

Date of publication: In both manuals, this is the date that appears on the title page of the treatise.

Revising editor's name substituted for edition: In the California Style Manual, if a treatise is identified with the name of a particular revising editor, substitute the name of the editor for the number of the edition in the parenthetical information (see the example for Williston on Contracts, above).

Cross-references: Cal. Style Manual § 3:1. Bluebook, Rules 15.1–15.4, pp. 103–107; Practitioners' Notes, P.1(b), p. 12.

§ 9:2   Rutter Group practice guides

In the California Style Manual, citations to Rutter Group practice guides are identical in format to other treatises with three exceptions: the volume number appears after the title, the publisher's name is included in parentheses, and paragraph numbers alone are sufficient.

In the Bluebook, there is no distinction between citing Rutter Group practice guides and other treatises or textbooks.

California Style Manual:

(Weil & Brown, Cal. Practice Guide: Civil Procedure Before Trial (The Rutter Group 1997) ¶ 3:10.)

(Croskey et al., Cal. Practice Guide: Insurance Litigation (The Rutter Group 1997) ¶¶ 17:3 to 17:4.)

(Friedman et al., Cal. Practice Guide: Landlord-Tenant (The Rutter Group 1998) ¶ 2:49.)

Bluebook:

1 Robert I. Weil & Ira A. Brown, California Practice Guide: Civil Procedure Before Trial ¶ 3:10 (1997).

2 H. Walter Croskey et al., California Practice Guide: Insurance Litigation ¶¶ 17:3–4 (1997).

1 C. Hugh Friedman et al., California Practice Guide: Landlord-Tenant ¶ 2:49 (1998).

Cross-references: Cal. Style Manual § 3:1. Bluebook, Rules 15.1–15.4, pp. 103–107; Practitioners' Notes, P.1(b), p. 12.

§ 9:3   Textbooks

In both manuals, textbooks are cited in accordance with the general rules set forth in §§ 9:1 and 9:2.

California Style Manual:

(York et al., Case Materials and Problems on General Practice Insurance Law (3d ed. 1994) p. 49.)

Bluebook:

Kenneth H. York et al., *Case Materials and Problems on General Practice Insurance Law* 49 (3d ed. 1994).

Cross-references: Cal. Style Manual § 3:1. Bluebook, Rules 15.1–15.4, pp. 103–107; Practitioners' Notes, P.1(b), p. 12.

§ 9:4   Supplements

In the California Style Manual, the volume number (if any) is followed by the author's last name (if any), a comma, the title of the treatise, and in parentheses, the publication date of the supplement and the abbreviation "supp.," then the chapter title (optional), followed by the section and/or page number references. When citing to the supplement alone, there is no need for the parent volume's edition and publication date.

In the Bluebook, the volume number is followed by the author's full name (if any), a comma, the title of the treatise underscored or italicized, another comma, section or page number references, and then in parentheses, the abbreviation "Supp." first, with the first letter capitalized, followed by the supplement's year of publication.

California Style Manual:

(Witkin, Cal. Criminal Law (1975 supp.) Diminished Capacity, p. 98.)

(3 Witkin, Summary of Cal. Law (1967 supp.) Corporations, p. 998.)

(4 Cal. Transactions Forms—Business Transactions (1999 supp.) § 29:13.).

It is appropriate to consider Witkin, California Criminal Law (1975 supp.) Diminished Capacity, page 98, when attempting to resolve this issue.

Bluebook:

Bernard E. Witkin, *California Criminal Law* 98 (Supp. 1975).

3 Bernard E. Witkin, *Summary of California Law* 998 (Supp. 1967).

4 *Cal. Transactions Forms—Business Transactions* § 29:13 (Supp. 1999).

It is appropriate to consider Witkin, *California Criminal Law* 98 (Supp. 1975), when attempting to resolve this issue.

Cross-references: Cal. Style Manual § 3:1[B]. Bluebook, Rule 3.2(c), p. 34; Rule 15.4(e), p. 107.

§ 9:5 Updates

In the California Style Manual, the edition and publication date of the main treatise are followed by a second parenthetical that includes the release or revision date of the looseleaf replacement page.

In the Bluebook no distinction is made between treatise supplements and updates. However, the following example is consistent with standard Bluebook format.

California Style Manual:

(4 Ballantine & Sterling, Cal. Corporation Laws (4th ed. 1998) § 484.02, p. 49–54 (rel. 72-4/99).)

Bluebook:

4 Henry Winthrop Ballantine & Graham Lee Sterling, *California Corporation Laws* § 484.02, pp. 49–54 (4th ed. 1998) (rel. 72-4/99).

§ 9:6 Both text and supplement

In the California Style Manual, if the supplement's page or section number corresponds to the main volume, use an ampersand, the year of the supplement, and the abbreviation "supp." after the publication date of the main volume.

In the Bluebook, the edition and publication date of the main volume are cited, followed by the abbreviation "Supp." and the supplement's year of publication.

California Style Manual:

(2 Witkin, Cal. Evidence (3d ed. 1986 & 1999 supp.) Public Policy, § 1401A, p. 290.)

Bluebook:

2 Bernard E. Witkin, *California Evidence* § 1401A, p. 290 (3d ed. 1986 & Supp. 1199).

Cross-references: Cal. Style Manual § 3:1[C]. Bluebook, Rule 3.2(c), p. 34.

§ 9:7   Subsequent references to treatises

Subsequent references to treatises require a short citation form. The goal of short citations is to provide sufficient information so that the reader may easily refer to the source without having to search back for the parent citation, yet be brief enough so as to not be too distracting.

Repeat citation directly follows in same paragraph: In the California Style Manual, when the repeat citation directly follows the parent citation in the same paragraph, use "*ibid.*" and the page number instead of repeating the full citation. ("*Ibid.*" means "in the same place" and should only be used if the exact same citation is repeated.) If only the point page is different in the repeat citation, use "*id.* at" and the page number instead.

In the Bluebook, when the repeat citation directly follows the parent citation in the same paragraph, use "*id.*" instead of repeating the full citation. If the point page is different in the repeat citation, use "*id.* at" and the page number or "Witkin at" and the page number instead of repeating the full citation.

California Style Manual:

Parent citation:

(5 Miller & Starr, Current Law of Cal. Real Estate (2d ed. 1998) Escrows, § 5:24, p. 342.)

Identical repeat citation directly following parent citation in same paragraph:

(*Ibid.*)

Repeat citation with point page different than inception page, but directly following parent citation in same paragraph:

(*Id.* at p. 362.)

Bluebook:

Parent citation:

5 Harry D. Miller & Marvin B. Starr, *Current Law of California Real Estate* § 5:24, p. 342 (2d ed. 1998).

Identical repeat citation in same paragraph:

Id.

Repeat citation with point page different from inception page:

Id. at 362.

Miller & Starr at 362.

Repeat citation does not directly follow parent citation: In both manuals, if the repeat citation does not directly follow the parent citation, give the volume number of the treatise (if any), the author's last name, the title of the treatise and the word "*supra.*" followed by the section number and/or the page number.

California Style Manual:

(5 Miller & Starr, Current Law of Cal. Real Estate, *supra,* § 5:24, p. 342.)

Bluebook:

5 Miller & Starr, *Current Law of California Real Estate, supra* § 5:24, p. 342.

Cross-references: Cal. Style Manual § 3:1[C]. Bluebook, Rule 15.8.1, pp. 110–111.

Citation to different volume: In the California Style Manual, when the publication dates are the same, use "*supra*" references to different volumes. If the year of publication in the volume being cited is different from the year of the parent citation, treat the cite as an initial citation.

In the Bluebook, the rule is similar to the California Style Manual, however, "*infra*" is used interchangeably with "*supra.*"

California Style Manual:

Publication dates are the same:

(2 Witkin, Summary of Cal. Law (9th ed. 1987) Agency, § 135, p. 131.).

(3 Witkin, *supra,* Secured Transactions in Real Property, § 86, p. 369.)

Publication dates are different:

(2 Witkin, Summary of Cal. Law (9th ed. 1987) Agency, § 135, p. 131.).

(5 Witkin, Summary of Cal. Law (8th ed. 1992) Torts, § 174, p. 332.).

Bluebook:

Publication dates are the same:

2 Bernard E. Witkin, *Summary of California Law*, Agency § 135, p. 131
  (9th ed. 1987).

3 Witkin, *supra Secured Transactions in Real Property* § 86, p. 369.

Publication dates are different:

2 Bernard E. Witkin, *Summary of California Law* § 135, p. 131 (9th ed.
  1987).

5 Bernard E. Witkin, *Summary of California Law* § 174, p. 332 (8th ed.
  1992).

Cross-references: Cal. Style Manual § 3:1[C]. Bluebook, Rules 4,
4.1, pp. 40–43; Rules 15.8, 15.8.1, pp. 110–111.

Use of "hereafter" and "hereinafter": In situations where the use
of "*supra*" would be unwieldly or where the usual short cite form may be
confusing, a unique shortened form may be introduced. The California
Style Manual places the word "hereafter" in a parenthetical containing the
short cite, which is often just the author's name followed by "at p." and the
page number.

The Bluebook places the short cite in brackets and introduces it with
the word "hereinafter." Thereafter, the short cite is followed by a comma
and either "*id.*" or "*supra.*"

California Style Manual:

Parent citation:

(Croskey & Kaufman, Cal. Practice Guide: Insurance Litigation (The Rutter
  Group 1998) ¶ 12:1281 (hereafter Croskey).)

Repeat citation:

Croskey at ¶ 12:1295.

Bluebook:

Parent citation:

(H. Walter Croskey & Marcus M. Kaufman, 2 *California Practice Guide: Insurance Litigation* ¶ 12:1281 (Rutter Group 1998) [hereinafter Croskey].

Repeat citation:

Croskey, *supra,* ¶ 12:1295.

Cross-references: Cal. Style Manual § 3:1[D]. Bluebook, Practitioners' Notes, P.4(d), p. 16; Rule 4.2[b], pp. 42–43.

§ 9:8   Continuing Education of the Bar and Center for Judicial Education and Research publications

Main volume: In the California Style Manual, the volume number (if any) appears first, then the author's last name (if any), the title of the treatise or publication, and in parentheses, the abbreviation "Cont.Ed.Bar" or "CJER," and the year of publication, followed by a section symbol and/or page number.

The Bluebook makes no specific reference to either of these publications. The examples set forth below use the abbreviations adopted by the California Style Manual, but are consistent with Bluebook style for citing books.

Supplements: In the California Style Manual, the abbreviation "supp." in parentheses follows the year of publication. When citing an update, use the rule set forth in § 9:4 above.

In the Bluebook, the abbreviation "Supp." and the year the supplement was published are enclosed in parentheses.

California Style Manual:

(Cal. Criminal Law, Procedure and Practice (Cont.Ed.Bar 4th ed. 1998) §§ 22.1, 22.2, pp. 961–962.)

(Forming and Operating Cal. Limited Liability Companies (Cont.Ed.Bar. 1996) § 2:1.).

(Forming and Operating Cal. Limited Liability Companies (Cont.Ed.Bar. supp. 1999) § 3:5.).

(CJER Mandatory Criminal Jury Instructions Handbook (CJER 1996) § 3.8, p. 99.)

Bluebook:

California Criminal Law, Procedure and Practice, pp. 961–962 (Cont. Ed. Bar 1994).

Forming and Operating California Limited Liability Companies § 2:1 (Cont. Ed. Bar. 1996).

Forming and Operating California Limited Liability Companies § 3:5 (Cont. Ed. Bar Supp. 1999).

CJER Mandatory Criminal Jury Instructions Handbook § 3.8, p. 99 (CJER 1996).

Cross-references: Cal. Style Manual § 3:2. Bluebook, Rule 3.2(c), p. 34.

§ 9:9   Legal encyclopedias

In the California Style Manual, the volume number appears first, then the abbreviation for the title of the encyclopedia, the year of publication in parentheses, the subject, and a comma, followed by the section reference. Recall that no abbreviations are allowed when the citation forms an integral part of a sentence and is therefore enclosed in parentheses. No page number is necessary when citing an encyclopedia as a general reference.

In the Bluebook, the volume number appears first, the abbreviation for the legal encyclopedia in initial capital letters, the subject in italics or underscored, followed by the section reference and the year of publication in parentheses.

Table 18
Abbreviations for Legal Encyclopedias

Legal encyclopedia	California Style Manual	Bluebook
American Jurisprudence	Am.Jur., Am.Jur.2d	Am. Jur, Am. Jur. 2d.
California Jurisprudence	Cal.Jur., Cal.Jur.2d, Cal.Jur.3d	Cal. Jur., Cal. Jur. 2d, Cal. Jur. 3d.
Corpus Juris	C.J.	C.J.
Corpus Juris Secundum	C.J.S.	C.J.S.

Cross-references: Cal. Style Manual § 3:3[A], [B]. Bluebook, Rule 15.7(a), p. 109.

California Style Manual:

(77 C.J.S. (supp. 1936) Residence, p. 28, fn. 54.)

(50 Am.Jur.2d (1995) Larceny, § 67.)

Bluebook:

77 C.J.S. *Residence*, p. 28, fn. 54 (1936 Supp.)

50 Am. Jur. 2d *Larceny* § 67 (1995).

§ 9:10 Blackstone's Commentaries

In the California Style Manual, when citing the original work, the volume number appears first, then the title and page number. When citing an annotated reprint, the volume number appears first, then the title, and in parentheses the edition and year of publication followed by the page number.

In the Bluebook, when citing the original, the volume number appears first, followed by the title in italics or underscored, and then an asterisk and the page number. There is no space between the page number and the asterisk. The asterisk indicates that the page reference is to the original edition. When a "star page" is used, there is no need to cite the date and edition unless the cited text was added by an editor of a later edition.

California Style Manual:

2 Blackstone's Commentaries 152 *or*

2 Blackstone, Commentaries 152.

1 Tucker's Blackstone (1803) appen. note D, p. 297.

Gavit's Blackstone (1941), p. 359.

Bluebook:

2 William Blackstone, *Commentaries* *152.

1 *Tucker's Blackstone* (1803) app. note D, p. 297.

Gavit's Blackstone (1941), p. 359.

Cross-references: Cal. Style Manual § 3:3[C]. Bluebook, Rule 15.4(d), p. 107.

§ 9:11 Dictionaries

In the California Style Manual, the volume number appears first (if any), the title as it appears on the title page, and in parentheses, the edition and year of publication, and then the page reference. When the citation does not form an integral part of the sentence and is therefore enclosed in parentheses, use the abbreviation "Dict."

In the Bluebook, the title appears in italics or underscored, followed by the page number, and in parentheses, the edition and year of publication.

California Style Manual:

(Black's Law Dict. (6th ed. 1990) p. 745.)

As defined in Ballentine's Law Dictionary (3d ed. 1969) at page 322, the term "curtilege" means . . .

(1 Oxford English Dictionary (4th ed. 1993), p. 575.)

Bluebook:

Black's Law Dictionary 745 (6th ed. 1990).

As defined in *Ballentine's Law Dictionary* at page 322 (3d ed. 1969), the term "curtilege" means . . .

1 *Oxford English Dictionary* 575 (4th ed. 1993).

Cross-references: Cal. Style Manual § 3:4, Bluebook, Rule 15.7(a), p. 109.

§ 9:12 Jury instructions

In the California Style Manual, the abbreviation BAJI or CALJIC is used, followed by the abbreviation "No." for "number," and the jury instruction number. When citing to a jury instruction appearing in a supplement or pocket part, add the year the instruction was added or revised, its status (new, revised, or re-revised) followed by a second parenthetical containing the edition of the main volume, the year of publication, and the page on which the original instruction appears. When citing a comment, use the abbreviation "com." When citing to a note, no abbreviation is used.

In the Bluebook, no reference to jury instructions is made. Conform the rules set forth in the California Style Manual to the standard Bluebook format as illustrated below.

California Style Manual:

(BAJI No. 12.92 (1999 rev.) (8th ed. 1994).)

(Com. to BAJI No. 12.30 (8th ed. 1994) p. 124.)

(Note to BAJI No. 10.90 (8th ed. 1994) p. 578.)

(CALJIC No. 2.26 (6th ed. 1997).)

Bluebook:

BAJI No. 12.92 (1999 rev.) (8th ed. 1994).

Com. to BAJI No. 12.30, p. 124 (8th ed. 1994).

Note to BAJI No. 10.90, p. 578 (8th ed. 1994).

CALJIC No. 2.26 (6th ed. 1997).

Cross-references: Cal. Style Manual § 3.5.

§ 9:13 Restatements

In the California Style Manual, the title appears first followed by the section number. If the citation does not form an integral part of the sentence and is therefore enclosed in parentheses, the abbreviation "Rest." is used. If the citation is to the original Restatement, place a comma between "Rest." and the title. The following abbreviations are also allowed where the reference to the Restatement is enclosed in parentheses: "com." for comment, "illus." for "illustration," "appen." for "appendix," and "p." for "page." When citing material that appears in an appendix, insert the abbreviation "appen." in parentheses after the title and before the section reference.

In the Bluebook, the title appears in italics or underscored followed by the section number, and reference to "cmt." for "comment" or "illus." for "illustration," and then the year of publication in parentheses. If the material appears in an appendix, the abbreviation "app." appears last in the parenthetical information.

California Style Manual:

(Rest.2d Trusts, § 285.)

(Rest.3d Unfair Competition, § 39.)

(Rest., Contracts (appen.) § 59, com. d, illus. 2, p. 926.)

Bluebook:

Restatement (Second) of Trusts § 285 (1957).

Restatement (Third) of Unfair Competition § 39 (1995).

Restatement of Contracts § 59, cmt. d, illus. 2, p. 926 (1993 App.).

Cross-references: Cal. Style Manual § 3:6. Bluebook, Rule 3.5, p. 39.

§ 9:14 Annotated reporters

General rule: Both manuals use the same abbreviations to cite to the American Law Reports (A.L.R.) for the first through fifth series, and for the federal series (A.L.R.Fed.). However, the Bluebook inserts a space between "A.L.R." and "Fed." in its abbreviation of the federal series.

In the California Style Manual, the title of the annotated reporter is prefaced by "Annot." or "Annotation," the annotation title (optional), the volume's year of publication, the volume number, the abbreviation for the reporter (e.g., "A.L.R."), and the inception page. Section and footnote references may be included.

When citing a supplement, insert the year the supplement was published followed by the abbreviation "supp." in parentheses after the page number of the main volume.

In the Bluebook, the author's full name appears first followed by a comma, the word "Annotation," the annotation title in italics, a comma, the volume number, the abbreviation of the annotation reporter title, followed by the page number. The citation ends with the year of publication, in parentheses.

When citing a supplement, insert an ampersand after the year the main volume was published, the abbreviation "Supp.," and the year the supplement was published.

California Style Manual:

(Annot., Delay Between Seizure of Personal Property by Federal Government and Institution of Proceedings for Forfeiture Thereof as Violative of Fifth Amendment Due Process Requirements (1984) 69 A.L.R.Fed. 373, and later cases (1999 supp.) p. 26.)

(Annot., Sufficiency of Proof that Mental or Neurological Condition Complained of Resulted from Accident or Incident in Suit Rather than from Pre-Existing Condition (1965) 2 A.L.R.3d 487.)

(Annot., What Constitutes "Claim Arising in a Foreign Country" under 28 U.S.C.A. § 2680(k) Excluding Such Claims from Federal Tort Claims Act (1999) 158 A.L.R.Fed. 137).

Bluebook:

Annotation, *Delay Between Seizure of Personal Property by Federal Government and Institution of Proceedings for Forfeiture Thereof as Violative of Fifth Amendment Due Process Requirements*, 69 A.L.R. Fed. 373 (1984 & Supp. 1999).

Annotation, *Sufficiency of Proof that Mental or Neurological Condition Complained of Resulted from Accident or Incident in Suit Rather than from Pre-Existing Condition*, 2 A.L.R.3d 487 (1965).

Kurtis A. Kemper, Annotation, *What Constitutes "Claim Arising in a Foreign Country" under 28 U.S.C.A. § 2680(k), Excluding Such Claims from Federal Tort Claims Act*, 158 A.L.R. Fed. 137 (1999).

Cross-references: Cal. Style Manual § 3:7[C]. Bluebook, Rule 16.5.5, p. 118; Rule 3.2(c), p. 34.

§ 9:15 Law reviews and bar journals

General rule: In the California Style Manual, the last name of the author appears first followed by a comma, then the title of the article in italics or underscored, a comma, the date, the volume number, the abbreviation of the periodical's title, the inception page, and the point page (if appropriate). If two authors are being cited, both last names are used, connected with an ampersand or "and." If more than two authors are being cited, the abbreviation "et al." is used after the first author's name, and no other authors are cited. When citing a note or comment, use "Note" or "Comment" instead of the author's last name.

In the Bluebook, the full name of the author appears, followed by the article title in italics, a comma, the volume number of the periodical, the abbreviation of the periodical title in initial capital letters, and the page number. The year of publication follows last, in parentheses. When a note or comment is cited, the word "Note" or "Comment" follows the author's name.

Table 19
Abbreviations of Frequently Cited Law Reviews and Bar Journals

Periodical title	California Style Manual	Bluebook
California Law Review	Cal. L.Rev.	Cal. L. Rev.
California Western Law Review	Cal. Western L.Rev.	Cal. W. L. Rev.
Ecology Law Quarterly	Ecology L.Q.	Ecology L.Q.
Harvard Civil Rights-Civil Liberties Law Review	Harv.C.R.-C.L. L.Rev.	Harv. C.R.-C.L. L. Rev.
Harvard Law Review	Harv. L.Rev.	Harv. L. Rev.
Hastings Constitutional Law Quarterly	Hastings Const. L.Q.	Hastings Const. L.Q
Hastings Law Journal	Hastings L.J.	Hastings L.J.
Loyola University of Los Angeles Law Review	Loyola L.A. L.Rev.	Loy. L.A. L. Rev.
Pacific Law Journal	Pacific L.J.	Pacific L.J.
Pepperdine Law Review	Pepperdine L.Rev.	Pepp. L. Rev.
San Diego Law Review	San Diego L.Rev.	San Diego L. Rev.
Santa Clara Law Review	Santa Clara L.Rev.	Santa Clara L. Rev.
Southern California Law Review	So.Cal. L.Rev.	S. Cal. L. Rev.
Southwestern University Law Review	Sw.U. L.Rev.	Sw. U. L. Rev.
Stanford Law Review	Stan. L.Rev.	Stan. L. Rev.
University of California at Los Angeles Law Review	UCLA L.Rev.	UCLA L. Rev.
University of California at Davis Law Review	U.C. Davis L.Rev.	U.C. Davis L. Rev.
University of San Francisco Law Review	U.S.F. L.Rev.	U.S.F. L. Rev.

California Style Manual:

(Cooper, *Towards a New Architecture: Creative Problem Solving and the Evolution of Law* (1998) 34 Cal. Western L.Rev. 297 (hereafter Cooper).)

(Note, *Women's Jury Service: Right of Citizenship or Privilege of Difference?*, (1994) 46 Stan. L.Rev. 1115 (hereafter Women's Jury Service).)

(Comment, *The Quality of First Amendment Speech* (1998) 20 Hastings L.J.275 (hereafter First Amendment Speech).)

Bluebook:

James M. Cooper, *Towards a New Architecture: Creative Problem Solving and the Evolution of Law*, 34 Cal. W. L. Rev. 297 (1998) [hereinafter Cooper].

Joanna L. Grossman, Note, *Women's Jury Service: Right of Citizenship or Privilege of Difference?*, 46 Stan. L. Rev. 1115 (1994) [hereinafter Grossman].

Randall P. Bezanson, Comment, *The Quality of First Amendment Speech*, 20 Hastings L.J. 275 (1998) [hereinafter Bezanson].

Cross-references: Cal. Style Manual § 3.8. Bluebook, Rule 16.5.1(a), p. 115; Table T.13, pp. 299–317.

Subsequent references to law reviews and bar journals: In the California Style Manual, using short cites to repeat citations to a law review article or bar journal in the same document are allowed. Customarily short cites are to the author's last name or a shortened version of the title followed by the point page.

In the Bluebook, "*id.*" is used when the subsequent reference immediately follows the parent citation indicating any page difference. Otherwise, the author's last name is used before the word "*supra.*" If no author's name is used, citation is made to a shortened version of the title instead, followed by the page number.

California Style Manual:

(Cooper at 299.)

(Women's Jury Service at 1120.)

(First Amendment Speech at 301.)

Bluebook:

Id. at 299.

Grossman, *supra* at 1120.

Bezanson, *supra* at 301.

Cross-references: Cal. Style Manual § 3:8. Bluebook, Rule 16.6, pp. 119–120.

§ 9:16 Topical law reporters and services

General rule: In the California Style Manual, there is no uniform citation style for topical reporters and services because they are produced in a variety of formats. However, to the extent that it is practicable, citation is made to : (1) a description of the item cited (e.g., the author and italicized title, where applicable); (2) a parenthetical listing the publisher (optional) and the date of publication; (3) the volume and/or issue number; and (4) the abbreviated publication title and page, paragraph, or section designation. (For example, "law reporter" is abbreviated as "L.Rptr." and "law reports" as "L.Rep.") Abbreviations of the title of the service or topical reporter are acceptable regardless of whether the cite is an integral part of the sentence or is enclosed in parentheses.

In the Bluebook, the author's full name (if available) appears first, then the title of the article or commentary in italics, followed by the volume of the topical law reporter or service, the abbreviated name of the reporter or service, an abbreviation for the name of the publisher in parentheses, the page or section reference, and the date or year of the publication in parentheses. For a list of abbreviations commonly used in referring to services, see the Bluebook, Table T.15, pp. 319–324.

California Style Manual:

(Woods, *To Dismiss or Not Dismiss: That Is the Question* (Cont.Ed.Bar. 1980) 2 Civ. Litigation Rptr. 109, 112.)

(Conran, *Point: Consumers Should Be Turned on by "Poolco,"* 15 Sum-Cal Reg. L. Rptr. 2–3.)

Bluebook:

M. Woods, *To Dismiss or Not Dismiss: That Is the Question,* 2 Civ. Litigation Rep. (Cont. Ed. Bar.) 109, 112 (1980).

(Jim Conran, *Point: Consumers Should Be Turned on by "Poolco,"* 15 Sum.-Cal. Reg. L. Rep. 2–3 (Spring 1995).

Cross-references: Cal. Style Manual § 3:9. Bluebook, Rule 18.1, pp. 129–130, Table T.15, p. 319.

§ 9:17 Legal citation manuals

General rule: In the California Style Manual, legal citation manuals are cited by title, the edition and date of publication in parentheses, and the section number. Page references are acceptable if they assist the reader in quickly locating the material cited. When the citation forms an integral part of a sentence, no parentheses or abbreviations are used. When the citation is enclosed in parentheses, the customary abbreviations are allowed (e.g., "Cal." for "California").

In the Bluebook, the form for citing either manual is not specifically addressed. The form used below is consistent with standard Bluebook form for citing treatises.

California Style Manual:

(Cal. Style Manual (4th ed. 2000) § 3:10.)

As required by section 3:1 of the California Style Manual, *supra*, the title of a service is . . .

(The Bluebook: A Uniform System of Citation (16th ed. 1996) § 18, p. 129.)

In contrast, the *Bluebook*, *supra*, section 18, page 129 does not require . . .

Bluebook:

Edward W. Jessen, *California Style Manual* § 3:10 (4th ed. 2000).

As required by section 3:10 of the *California Style Manual*, *supra*, the title of the service is . . .

The Bluebook: A Uniform System of Citation § 18, p. 129 (16th ed. 1996). In contrast, the Bluebook, *supra* § 18, p. 129, does not require . . .

Cross-references: Cal. Style Manual § 3:10. Bluebook, *see* Practitioners' Notes, P.1(b), p. 12.

§ 9:18 Magazines

General rule: In both manuals, articles appearing in legal magazines are cited in accordance with the format prescribed for law reviews and journals.

California Style Manual:

(Susan M. Heinrich-Wells, *The Enforceability of Liability Releases in High-Risk Sports* (June 1998) 21 Los Angeles Lawyer 26.)

(Susan E. Davis, *The Bar By the Bay* (Dec. 1997) California Lawyer 41.)

In *The Enforceability of Liability Releases in High-Risk Sports* (June 1998), 21 Los Angeles Lawyer 26, the author attempted to dispel . . .

Bluebook:

Susan M. Heinrich-Wells, *The Enforceability of Liability Releases in High-Risk Sports*, 21 Los Angeles Lawyer 26 (June 1998).

Susan E. Davis, *The Bar By the Bay*, California Lawyer, Dec. 1997 at p. 41.

In *The Enforceability of Liability Releases in High-Risk Sports*, 21 Los Angeles Lawyer 26 (June 1998), the author attempted to dispel . . .

Cross-references: Cal. Style Manual § 3:11. Bluebook, Rule 16, pp. 112–115.

§ 9:19 Legal newspapers

In the California Style Manual, the name of the author, if available, is listed, followed by the title of the article in italics, the title of the publication, the full date in parentheses, and the page number (if any), and column number (optional).

In the Bluebook, the full name of the author is followed by the title of the article in italics, the abbreviated title of the publication, a comma, the full date of publication, a section reference (if any), and the page reference to the first page of the article.

California Style Manual:

(Crowley, *Pecos Crew Remembers Seven Lost Servicemen*, San Diego Daily
Transcript (December 18, 1999) p. B5.)

(Krueger, *Judge Expects to Miss Several Months at Least*, L.A. Daily J.
(December 14, 1999) p. B2.)

Bluebook:

James Crowley, *Pecos Crew Remembers Seven Lost Servicemen*, San Diego
Daily Transcript, December 18, 1999, p. B5.

Ann Krueger, *Judge Expects to Miss Several Months at Least*, L.A. Daily J.,
December 14, 1999, p. B2.

Cross-references: Cal. Style Manual § 3:12. Bluebook, Rule 16.4, p.
114; Practitioners' Notes, P.1(b), p. 12.

CHAPTER 9
—Notes—

CHAPTER 9
—Notes—

CHAPTER 10

GENERAL RULES FOR CAPITALIZATION, QUOTES, NUMBERS, ITALICS, AND PUNCTUATION

C. NUMBERS AND ITALICS

D. PUNCTUATION

A. CAPITALIZATION

§ 10:1   References to courts

General rule: In both manuals, the full name of any court is capitalized (e.g., the Superior Court of San Diego County, Central Division). References to the United States Supreme Court are always capitalized, as is the word "court" in subsequent references. General references to a court (e.g., "this issue has never been addressed by a court of appeal or high court in any state") are not capitalized.

In the California Style Manual, references to state supreme courts and courts of appeal (including the district and division designations) are capitalized. Subsequent references to the full or partial name of these courts are also capitalized (e.g., "the Court held . . ." or "Division Two has held otherwise").

In the Bluebook, references to state supreme courts and courts of appeal are not capitalized unless referring to a specific court. The word "court" is also capitalized when referring to the court that will be receiving the pleading, motion, or other document.

California Style Manual:

In 1997, the United States Supreme Court decided *Saratoga Fishing Co. v. J.M. Martinac & Co.* (1997) 520 U.S. 875 [117 S.Ct. 1783]. In *Saratoga*, the Court determined that the *East River* limitation on damages applied . . .

In *Buss v. Superior Court* (1997) 16 Cal.4th 35 [65 Cal.Rptr.2d 366], our Supreme Court opined . . . . Since *Buss*, the Court of Appeal for the Fourth District, Division 2, has extended the "right of reimbursement" for mixed actions to those actions that . . . . However, the Fourth District has refused to apply this rule to cases where . . . .

The United States Court of Appeals, Eighth Circuit has never had the occasion to determine this issue.

Appellate courts have reached different conclusions in this regard, and no state high court has ever addressed this issue.

Small claims courts have no jurisdiction to adjudicate claims where the amount in dispute exceeds $5,000.

The trial court in *Corso* granted summary judgment upholding the enforceability of the release of liability.

Defendant respectfully requests this court to enter an order prohibiting . . .

Bluebook:

In 1997, the United States Supreme Court decided *Saratoga Fishing Co. v. J.M. Martinac & Co.*, 520 U.S. 875, 117 S. Ct. 1783 (1997). In *Saratoga*, the Court determined that the *East River* limitation on damages applied . . . . (*Same as Cal. Style Manual but for form of citation.*)

In *Buss v. Superior Court*, 16 Cal. 4th 35, 65 Cal. Rptr. 2d 366 (1997), our Supreme Court opined . . . . Since *Buss*, the Court of Appeal for the Fourth District, Division 2, has extended the "right of reimbursement" for mixed actions to those actions that . . . . However, the Fourth District has refused to apply this rule to cases where . . . . (*Same as Cal. Style Manual but for form of citation.*)

The United States Court of Appeals, Eighth Circuit, has never had the occasion to determine this issue. (*Same as Cal. Style Manual.*)

Appellate courts have reached different conclusions in this regard, and no state high court has ever addressed this issue. (*Same as Cal. Style Manual.*)

Small claims courts have no jurisdiction to adjudicate claims where the amount in dispute exceeds $5,000. (*Same as Cal. Style Manual.*)

The trial court in *Corso* granted summary judgment upholding the enforceability of the release of liability. (*Same as Cal. Style Manual.*)

Defendant respectfully requests this Court to enter an order prohibiting . . .

Cross-references: Cal. Style Manual §§ 4:1, 4:2. Bluebook, Practitioners' Notes, P.6, p. 17, and Rule 8, p. 51.

§ 10:2 Party designations

General rule: In the California Style Manual, a party's designation (e.g., "plaintiff," "defendant," "appellant," "respondent," etc.) is not ordinarily capitalized. This is true regardless of whether the designation is used alone or in conjunction with the party's name.

There are two exceptions to this general rule: (1) when a party is the People of the State of California, use "People" as its designation; (2) when a party's name is long and cumbersome, use a short form (i.e., following the party's name, enclose in parentheses the word "hereafter" and a short name for the party, such as "plaintiff," or one or two words identifying the party).

In the Bluebook, party designations are ordinarily capitalized except when a party's designation does not refer to a party before the court.

California Style Manual:

In the instant case, defendant Jones knowingly and voluntarily . . .

This reply is submitted in response to plaintiff's opposition to defendant's motion for summary adjudication.

In this case, defendant Montrose Air-Conditioning, Heating and Ventilation, Inc. (hereafter Defendant) did not timely file an answer. Consequently, Defendant is not in a position to complain of . . .

or

In this case, defendant Montrose Air-Conditioning, Heating and Ventilation, Inc. (hereafter Montrose) did not timely file an answer. Consequently, Montrose is not in a position to complain of . . .

No demonstrative evidence was introduced by the People.

In *Corso*, the defendant voluntarily signed the release.

Bluebook:

In the instant case, Defendant Jones knowingly and voluntarily . . .

This Reply is submitted in response to Plaintiff's Opposition to Defendant's Motion for Summary Adjudication.

In this case, Defendant Montrose Air-Conditioning, Heating and Ventilation, Inc. did not file a timely answer. Consequently, Defendant is not in a position to complain of . . .

or

In this case, Defendant Montrose Air-Conditioning, Heating and Ventilation, Inc. [hereinafter Montrose] did not file a timely answer. Consequently, Montrose is not in a position to complain of . . .

No demonstrative evidence was introduced by the People.

In *Corso*, the defendant voluntarily signed the release.

Cross-references: Cal. Style Manual § 4:11. Bluebook, Practitioners' Notes, P.6, p. 17; Rule 4.1(b), pp. 42–43.

§ 10:3   Titles of court documents

General rule: In the California Style Manual, no particular reference is made to capitalizing the title of documents submitted to a court in legal memoranda. However, since capitalizing headings and subheadings in documents submitted to the court is in the discretion of the author, it is inferable that capitalizing the titles of court-submitted documents in legal memoranda are also in the discretion of the author.

In the Bluebook, the title of previous documents filed in the pending action are capitalized in legal memoranda and other court documents. Subsequent references to the title of documents may be abbreviated at the discretion of the author. Articles and prepositions may be omitted from the abbreviated title.

Generic references to names of courts or discovery documents are not capitalized.

Bluebook:

In her Separate Statement of Undisputed Facts in Support of Motion for Summary Adjudication, Plaintiff fails to set forth any facts supporting her theory that Defendant's First Affirmative Defense is without merit. Moreover, she is unable to allege any *undisputed* facts that Defendant did not own the property at the time of the incident. (Pl.'s Sep. S. Undisp. Facts, p. 3).

Plaintiff's responses to the first set of requests for admissions were due on September 23, 1999.

Abbreviated citations to other court documents or legal memoranda: In the California Style Manual, no specific reference is made to the abbreviation of titles appearing in documents. It is therefore suggested that the rules set forth in the Bluebook be followed.

In the Bluebook, subsequent references to titles of documents filed previously in the same case may be abbreviated. The abbreviation is considered a citation and is enclosed in parentheses. When the citation appears in the middle of a sentence, the parentheses are enclosed with commas. When the citation appears at the end of a sentence, a period is placed after the closing parentheses. When the citation appears following a sentence as a separate citation sentence, the period is included within the parentheses. For abbreviations for court documents, see the Bluebook, Table T.8, p. 290.

Italics: Abbreviated citations to the record, declarations, exhibits, and the like are not italicized or underscored.

Bluebook:

The contract was signed by the Defendant. (White Decl. ¶ 3; Pl.'s Sep. S. Undisp. Facts, Ex. B ¶ 3.)

Contract negotiations took place in San Francisco, (R. at 12–13), but the contract was signed in Tucson, Arizona, (Jones Decl. ¶ 13).

Cross-references: Bluebook, Practitioners' Notes, P.7, pp. 18–19; Table T.8, pp. 290–291.

§ 10:4 Names of justices, judges, and jurors

General rule: In both manuals, titles that immediately precede or follow a person's name are capitalized, for example, Chief Justice Rehnquist; Judge Magistrate Leo Pappas; Victor Bianchini, Judge of the Superior Court of San Diego County, East Division; Juror William D. Wells.

Neither manual capitalizes titles that do not refer to a particular justice, judge, or juror. For example, the word "juror" is not capitalized in the following sentence: "A juror, empanelled on July 30, 1998, was dismissed for health reasons." Nor is the phrase "superior court judge" capitalized in the following sentence: "He was a superior court judge from 1987 until he retired in 1999."

In the California Style Manual, certain "formal, complete titles," such as Chief Justice, Attorney General, or State Public Defender are capitalized even when not coupled with a name. This is contrary to the Bluebook, which does not make this exception to the general rule stated above.

In the Bluebook, references to justices of the United States Supreme Court are always capitalized.

California Style Manual:

She was the first female justice of the United States Supreme Court.

In California, the Attorney General is empowered by the . . .

The Chief Justice of the United States Supreme Court is responsible . . .

Bluebook:

She was the first female Justice of the United States Supreme Court.

In California, the attorney general is empowered by the . . .

The Chief Justice of the United States Supreme Court is responsible . . .

Cross-references: Cal. Style Manual § 4:3[A], [B]. Bluebook, Rule 8, pp. 50–52.

§ 10:5 Prosecutors and other attorneys

General rule: In both manuals, nouns that refer to people, officials, or government offices are capitalized when they identify specific persons, officials, government offices, or bodies. Generic references to them are not capitalized.

California Style Manual and *Bluebook:*

Attorney General Davis was a staunch advocate of . . .

A public defender is an attorney employed by the county to protect . . .

Public Defender Hayden Estes

The San Diego Public Defender's Office is closed for the holiday.

The Madera County Public Defender

Janis White, an assistant attorney general

Janis White, Assistant Attorney General

Jonathan Goldman, defendant's attorney

Defense Attorney Jonathan Goldman

Cross-references: Cal. Style Manual § 4:3[C]. Bluebook, Rule 8, pp. 50–52.

§ 10:6 Administrative agencies, bodies, and districts

General rule: In both manuals, nouns that refer to administrative agencies, bodies, and districts are capitalized when they identify a specific administrative agency, body or district. Generic references to them are not capitalized.

In the California Style Manual, nouns such as "commission," "department," "district," or "board" are not capitalized when standing alone, even when they refer to a specific entity. However, when using an abbreviation for a short cite, the abbreviation may be capitalized at the author's discretion.

California Style Manual:

The Environmental Protection Agency (hereafter EPA) is headquartered in San Francisco. The EPA is responsible for enforcing the rules promulgated by various governmental agencies designed to protect our natural resources.

or

The Environmental Protection Agency is headquartered in San Francisco. The agency is responsible for enforcing the rules promulgated by various governmental agencies designed to protect our natural resources.

The tenants are responsible for submitting income statements to the State Board of Equalization (hereafter SBE) on an annual basis. The SBE is a state agency that monitors the . . .

or

The tenants are responsible for submitting income statements to the State Board of Equalization on an annual basis. The board is a state agency that monitors the . . .

The respondent district filed a timely notice of appeal, however the . . .

Bluebook:

The Environmental Protection Agency [hereinafter EPA] is headquartered in San Francisco. The EPA is responsible for enforcing the rules promulgated by various governmental agencies designed to protect our natural resources. (*Same as Cal. Style Manual but for the use of "(hereafter . . .)" instead of "[hereinafter . . .]."*)

or

The Environmental Protection Agency is headquartered in San Francisco. The Agency is responsible for enforcing the rules promulgated by various governmental agencies designed to protect our natural resources.

The tenants are responsible for submitting income statements to the State Board of Equalization [hereinafter SBE] on an annual basis. The SBE is a state agency that monitors the . . .

or

The tenants are responsible for submitting income statements to the State
  Board of Equalization on an annual basis. The Board is a state agency
  that monitors the . . .

The Respondent District filed a timely notice of appeal, however the . . .

Cross-references: Cal. Style Manual § 4:4. Bluebook, Rule 8,
pp. 50–52.

§ 10:7   Executive and administrative officers

General rule: In both manuals, nouns describing a particular government officer are always capitalized even when standing alone (contrary
to agencies, bodies, or districts as described in § 10:6).

Executive officers: In the California Style Manual, titles such as
President, Vice-President, or Governor that denote unusual preeminence or
distinction are capitalized when used as a substitute for the name. Subordi-
nate executive or administrative officers' titles, such as "assistant city manager," are never capitalized, nor are the nouns denoting corporate or
organizational officers in the private sector.

In the Bluebook, titles such as President, Vice-President, or Governor
are always capitalized because they refer to a particular executive officer.

Federal and state officers: In the California Style Manual, titles of
local officials, such as "sheriff," "city manager," "water commissioner," and
"mayor," are not capitalized unless they are used in an adjective form preceding the officeholder's name or with the name of a political subdivision.

In the Bluebook, no distinction is made between officials.

California Style Manual:

In his tenure, President Clinton has withstood challenges that . . . .
  Nevertheless, the President has maintained a steady course.

Quick to criticize his own personnel, Sheriff J. D. Smith is not viewed by the
  department as one who takes responsibility . . . . It is not unlikely that
  the sheriff will resign at the end of the . . . .

The president of Gemology America is scheduled to speak on . . .

Bluebook:

In his tenure, President Clinton has withstood challenges that . . . .
Nevertheless, the President has maintained a steady course. (*Same as Cal. Style Manual but for different reasons.*)

Quick to criticize his own personnel, Sheriff J. D. Smith is not viewed by the Department as one who takes responsibility . . . . It is not unlikely that the Sheriff will resign at the end of the . . . .

The President of Gemology America is scheduled to speak on . . .

Cross-references: Cal. Style Manual § 4:5. Bluebook, Rule 8, pp. 50–52.

§ 10:8 Legislative bodies and officers

General rule: In both manuals, nouns referring to a specific county, state, or national legislative office are capitalized.

California Style Manual and Bluebook:

The Social Security Administrator

In 1995, the congressional hearings were held approximately . . .

The Senate

The House of Representatives

There is no requirement that the lower house reach a consensus . . .

The California Legislature

The City Counsel of San Diego

The Board of Supervisors of Marin County

Cross-references: Cal. Style Manual § 4:6. Bluebook, Rule 8, pp. 50–52.

§ 10:9 States, counties, cities, towns, and geographic terms

General rule: In the California Style Manual, words such as "state," "city," "town," etc. are capitalized when they are part of a proper name. In the case of geographic terms such as "the Bay Area," terms that are commonly used as proper names are also capitalized. Those that do not apply to a single geographic area or that have not been commonly accepted as a proper name are not. Finally, when used in a short cite, an author may chose to abbreviate these words using initial capital letters.

In the Bluebook, in addition to capitalizing words such as "state," "city," "town," etc. when part of a proper name, these words are also capitalized if they modify a word that is capitalized or when referring to a state as a governmental actor or party to litigation.

California Style Manual:

The State of California (hereafter State)

The State Commissioner does not have the right to regulate or control . . .

In this case, defendant counties . . .

However, several eastern states adopt the minority view . . .

City of San Jose

East Coast lawyers are thought of as being . . .

In Southern California, county bar associations play a major role . . .

Bluebook:

The State of California [hereinafter State]

The State Commissioner does not have the right to regulate or control . . .

In this case, Defendant Counties . . . *(party to litigation)*

However, several eastern states adopt the minority view . . .

City of San Jose

East Coast lawyers are thought of as being . . .

In Southern California, county bar associations play a major role . . .

Cross-references: Cal. Style Manual § 4:7. Bluebook, Rule 8, pp. 50–52.

§ 10:10 Constitutions, amendments, statutes, and rules

General rule: In the California Style Manual, "constitution" is capitalized when referring to a specific constitution (state or federal). The words "article" or "clause" are not capitalized when used in text (e.g., "the supremacy clause of the United States Constitution") unless they are used as part of an actual title or heading. Words that are derivative of "constitution" are also not capitalized (e.g., "constitutional," "constitutionalize," "constitutionalist"). The words "federal" or "state" are not capitalized when prefacing "constitution."

In the Bluebook, nouns referring to any constitution in full or the United States Constitution are capitalized. In addition, nouns referring to any portion of the United States Constitution (e.g., Fourth Amendment) in a textual context (versus citation format) are capitalized, including the words "article," "section," and "clause." General references to constitutions are not capitalized.

California Style Manual:

United States Constitution

Constitution of the United States

The California Constitution

In this edition, constitutional interpretations appear in the last chapter.

The equal protection clause

The commerce clause

In article I, section 6 of the California Constitution

Fourteenth Amendment of the United States Constitution

Bluebook:

Constitution of the United States (*Same as Cal. Style Manual*)

The California Constitution (*Same as Cal. Style Manual*)

In this edition, constitutional interpretations appear in the last chapter. (*Same as Cal. Style Manual*)

The Equal Protection Clause

The Commerce Clause

In Article I, Section 6 of the California Constitution . . .

Fourteenth Amendment of the United States Constitution (*Same as Cal. Style Manual*)

Cross-references: Cal. Style Manual § 4:10[A]. Bluebook, Rule 8, pp. 50–52.

§ 10:11 Statutes, popular names, and government programs

General rule: In both manuals, official titles of statutes, popular names of acts, and government programs are capitalized.

Civil Discovery Act of 1986

Beverly-Killea Limited Liability Company Act

Aid to Families with Dependent Children

In the California Style Manual, subsequent references to a statute, act, or government program are not capitalized when standing alone (e.g., "The statute enumerates . . .") unless the author adopts "statute," "act," and the like as a short form abbreviation.

In the Bluebook, subsequent references referring to a specific statute, act, or government program are capitalized.

California Style Manual:

The Civil Discovery Act of 1986 has been amended in part. In 1972, the act was amended to . . .

The Beverly-Killea Limited Liability Company Act (hereafter Act) is a fairly recent statute. The Act was promulgated in . . .

Aid to Families with Dependent Children (hereafter AFDC).

Bluebook:

The Civil Discovery Act of 1986 has been amended in part. In 1972, the Act was amended to . . .

The Beverly-Killea Limited Liability Company Act [hereinafter Act] is a fairly recent statute. The Act was promulgated in . . .

Aid to Families with Dependent Children [hereinafter AFDC].

Cross-references: Cal. Style Manual § 4:10[B]. Bluebook, Rule 8, pp. 50–52.

§ 10:12 Familiar doctrines and unofficial or generic names of statutes

General rule: In the California Style Manual, the names of familiar doctrines or unofficial, generic names of statutes are not capitalized.

In the Bluebook, the treatment of familiar doctrines or unofficial generic names of statutes is not discussed. However, it would be consistent with Bluebook format to capitalize nouns that refer to a particular doctrine or statute, but not nouns that refer to general doctrines or statutes.

California Style Manual:

California's lemon law was enacted in the mid-eighties in response to . . .

The statutes of limitations prescribe the length of time within which . . .

The last clear chance doctrine came into being in connection with . . .

Bluebook:

California's Lemon Law was enacted in the mid-eighties in response to . . .

The statutes of limitations prescribe the length of time within which . . .

The Last Clear Chance Doctrine came into being in connection with . . .

Cross-references: Cal. Style Manual § 4:10[B]. Bluebook, see Rule 12.3.1, p. 76.

§ 10:13 Court rules

General rule: In the California Style Manual, the word "rule" is capitalized when part of a proper name but not when the word precedes a number.

In the Bluebook, the word "rule" is capitalized when it is part of a proper name and when it refers to a particular rule.

California Style Manual:

In that rule 6.2 of the Coordinated Rules of the Superior Court of San Diego County requires a party to file moving papers in connection with a request . . .

(Cal. Rules of Court, rule 977(d).)

Bluebook:

In that Rule 6.2 of the Coordinated Rules of the Superior Court of San Diego County requires a party to file moving papers in connection with a request . . .

Cal. Ct. R. 977(d).

Cross-references: Cal. Style Manual § 4:10[C]. Bluebook, Rule 12.8.3, p. 83.

B. QUOTED MATERIAL

§ 10:14　General rule

In both manuals, quoted material should correspond *exactly* to the original source in wording, spelling, capitalization, internal punctuation, and citation style. If a portion of a quote is distracting or not particularly relevant to the point being made, it may be omitted in accordance with the rules set forth below:

§ 10:15　Phrases or clauses

In both manuals, if only a phrase or fragment of a sentence is quoted, it is not necessary to indicate that the rest of the sentence has been omitted. For example:

> Pursuant to Section 2023, subdivision (a)(3), using discovery to cause "unwarranted annoyance, embarrassment, or oppression, or undue burden and expense" is sanctionable.

Since it is clear from the context that the language quoted is only a part of a quotation, there is no need to include any further indication of omission.

§ 10:16　Omissions—Beginning of a quoted sentence

In both manuals, where the language beginning a quote is omitted, the first letter of the first word of the quote is capitalized and enclosed in brackets. For example, the full quote is:

> "However, on motion with or without notice, the court, for good cause shown, may grant leave to a plaintiff to propound interrogatories at an earlier time."

When the beginning of the quote is omitted, the form should be as follows:

> "[T]he court, for good cause shown, may grant leave to a plaintiff to propound interrogatories at an earlier time."

Note that the inclusion of quotation marks, as well as capitalizing and bracketing the first letter of the first word, indicate that the beginning of the quotation has been omitted.

If the sentence did not begin with the quote, the form would be as follows:

> On the other hand, "the court for good cause shown, may grant leave to a plaintiff to propound interrogatories at an earlier time."

Cross-references: Cal. Style Manual § 4:13[A]. Bluebook, Rule 5.3(b)(i), p. 46.

§ 10:17 Omissions—Middle of a quoted sentence

In both manuals, use an ellipsis to indicate the omission of language from the middle of a quotation. Set off the ellipsis with a single space on either side.

> "[T]he court . . . may grant leave to a plaintiff to propound interrogatories at an earlier time."

> The lease provides that "Lessee shall maintain . . . the interior of the premises."

Cross-references: Cal. Style Manual § 4:13[B]. Bluebook, Rule 5.3(b)(ii), p. 46.

§ 10:18 Omissions—End of a quoted sentence

In both manuals, when language from the end of a quote is omitted, the omission is denoted by an ellipsis, followed by a period and the closing quotation mark.

> "[T]he court, for good cause shown, may grant leave to a plaintiff to propound interrogatories . . . ."

If the quote ends with a comma, a semicolon, or other punctuation, insert the ellipsis before the punctuation (ending the quote prior to the punctuation). If, for some reason, it is desirable to retain the punctuation, add the ellipsis after the punctuation.

> The court noted, "Good cause exists to allow plaintiff leave to propound interrogatories . . . ."

> The court noted, "Good cause exists to allow plaintiff to propound interrogatories before the statutory prescribed deadline, . . ."

> The court noted, "Good cause exists to allow plaintiff to propound interrogatories, . . ."

Cross-references: Cal. Style Manual § 4:13[C]. Bluebook, Rule 5.3(b)(iii), p. 46.

§ 10:19 Omissions—Text following a quoted sentence

In both manuals, if the sentence is a complete quote, there is no need to indicate that the text of the quote continues. However, if it is important to indicate that the quotation continues beyond the sentence quoted, an ellipsis after the period ending the sentence is used and a closing quotation mark. When quoting a sentence that follows the omitted text, an ellipsis between the end of the deleted text and the next sentence is used.

> The court noted, "Good cause exists." [or]
>
> The court noted, "Good cause exists. . . ."
>
> The court noted, "Good cause exists. . . . The order requested is hereby granted."

Cross-references: Cal. Style Manual § 4:13[D]. Bluebook, Rule 5.3(b)(iv), p. 46.

§ 10:20 Omissions—Significant portions of intervening material— From single paragraph

In the California Style Manual, when quoting two or more phrases or sentences from a single paragraph, each phrase or sentence must be enclosed in separate sets of quotation marks unless the second sentence immediately follows the first. If there is an intervening phrase or sentence, signal its omission by using an ellipsis. In the alternative, enclose each phrase or sentence in separate sets of quotation marks. Combining phrases from several sentences into a single quotation is frowned upon, even when the signals indicating omissions are included. Instead of combining the sentences, paraphrase the sentences with appropriate attribution or use separate quoted phrases. In the Bluebook, this matter is not specifically addressed.

Cross-references: Cal. Style Manual § 4:13[E][1].

§ 10:21 Omissions—Significant portions of intervening material— From consecutive paragraphs

In the California Style Manual, to indicate that a quoted sentence is from a different paragraph than the preceding quote, a paragraph symbol enclosed in brackets is inserted before the quote. This will signal the reader that the quote comes from a new paragraph of the original text.

In the Bluebook, this matter is not specifically addressed.

California Style Manual:

The relevant portion of the complaint alleges: "Johnson honored his obligation under the contract by tendering the purchase price in a timely fashion. [¶] Smith, however, failed to deliver the goods as promised. . . . [¶] Smith claims that performance was impossible due to unforeseeable circumstances."

Cross-references: Cal. Style Manual § 4:13[E][2].

§ 10:22 Omissions—Significant portions of intervening material— Omission of entire paragraphs

In the California Style Manual, to indicate that one or more paragraphs from a quoted passage are being omitted, two bracketed paragraph symbols separated by an ellipsis are used.

In the Bluebook, to indicate omission of one or more entire paragraphs, four periods are inserted on a new line. This rule applies only to quotations of 50 or more words. Quotation marks are dropped in favor of block-indenting the entire quote. Paragraph structure is then indicated by indenting the first line of each quoted paragraph. Quotations of 49 or fewer words are enclosed in quotation marks (rather than block-indented) and no paragraph structure need be indicated.

California Style Manual:

"Misuses of the discovery process include, but are not limited to the following: [¶] . . . [¶] 7. Disobeying a court order to provide discovery."

Bluebook:

"Misuses of the discovery process include, but are not limited to the following . . . . 7. Disobeying a court order to provide discovery."

Cross-references: Cal. Style Manual § 4:13[E][3]. Bluebook, Rule 5.4, p. 47.

§ 10:23 Omission—Of citations

In the California Style Manual, to indicate that citations contained in the quoted material have been omitted, substitute the words "[citation]" or "[citations]" for the omitted citation or string of citations.

141

California Style Manual:

"This doctrine, in one form or another, has been adopted in most
jurisdictions. [Citations.] However, . . ."

"All the indicia of discovery misuse are present, including evidence of
evasive responses to properly drafted requests for admissions [citations]
and disobeying a court order to provide discovery [citation]."

Using the phrase "citation omitted" or "internal citations omitted"
after the quotation's citation is also allowed as long as ellipses are used. This
practice should be avoided, however, because it does not tell the reader
whether the ellipses mean omitted text, omitted citations, or both.

"This is the rule prescribed by statute. . . . However, several common law
exceptions are still recognized." (See 6 Witkin, Cal. Procedure (4th ed.
1997) Court § 263, p. 391, citations omitted.)

In the Bluebook the same general rules apply, however, "(citation
omitted)" is used instead of "[citation]" and it is not necessary to use the
ellipses.

Bluebook:

"This doctrine, in one form or another, has been adopted in most
jurisdictions (citations omitted). However, . . ."

"All the indicia of discovery misuse are present, including evidence of
evasive responses to properly drafted requests for admissions (citations
omitted) and disobeying a court order to provide discovery (citations
omitted)."

"This is the rule prescribed by statute. . . . However, several common law
exceptions are still recognized." 6 Bernard E. Witkin, *California
Procedure* § 263 (4th ed. 1997) (citations omitted).

Cross-references: Cal. Style Manual § 4:13[F]. Bluebook, Rule
5.3, p. 45.

§ 10:24 Omission—Of footnotes

In the California Style Manual, to indicate the omission of footnotes,
the phrase "fn. omitted" or "fns. omitted" in brackets is used before the
closing quotation marks; or the phrase "fn. omitted" or "fns. omitted" is
enclosed in parentheses after the citation.

In the Bluebook, the same rule applies, however, no abbreviations are used and parentheses are used instead of brackets.

California Style Manual:

"California courts follow the majority rule. [Fn. omitted.]" (*Avilar v. Bandalini* (1998) 5 Cal.4th 10.)

or

"California courts follow the majority view." (*Avilar v. Bandalini* (1998) 5 Cal.4th 10, fn. omitted.)

Bluebook:

"California courts follow the majority rule." *Avilar v. Bandalini,* 5 Cal.4th 10 (1998) (footnote omitted).

In both manuals, if the quoted portion ends with a footnote, the author may terminate the quotation immediately before the footnote signal, in which case the footnote omission need not be noted.

Cross-references: Cal. Style Manual § 4:13[G]. Bluebook, Rule 5.3, p. 45.

§ 10:25 Omissions—Using bracketed substitutions

In both manuals, quoted material can be omitted and new material substituted for it, by enclosing the substitution in brackets when it is clear that the bracketed material replaces what appeared in the original. Ellipses are not used with the brackets.

California Style Manual **and** ***Bluebook:***

Original: "The California State Board of Equalization collects this information from every person or entity doing business in the State of California."

With substitution: "The [board] collects this information from every person or entity doing business in the State of California."

Cross-references: Cal. Style Manual § 4:14. Bluebook, Rule 5.2, p. 44.

§ 10:26 Quoting source containing error—Quote exactly

In both manuals, the general rule that the original text must be quoted *exactly* as it appears still applies even when the original text contains errors. When quoting material with errors, note that. the error is intentionally quoted or insert a correction in accordance with the rules set forth in §§ 10:27–10:29.

§ 10:27 Quoting source containing error—Misspelled words

In both manuals, insert "[*sic*]" after the error or substitute the correct spelling in brackets. Note, however, that while the California Style Manual italicizes "[*sic*]," the Bluebook does not.

California Style Manual:

"The court exercised it's [*sic*] discretion in granting the summary judgment motion."

"The court exercised [its] discretion in granting the summary judgment motion."

Bluebook:

"The court exercised it's [sic] discretion in granting the summary judgment motion."

"The court exercised [its] discretion in granting the summary judgment motion."

Cross-references: Cal. Style Manual § 4:15[B]. Bluebook, Rule 5.2, p. 44.

§ 10:28 Quoting source containing error—Grammatical errors

In both manuals, when the sentence being quoted is grammatically incorrect or some other obvious flaw prevents a smooth reading, indicate the error by inserting "[*sic*]" immediately following the error. In the California Style Manual, "(*Sic.*)" may also be used after the quotation.

California Style Manual:

"The judgment were [*sic*] entered on December 27, 1999."

"The fourth cause of action allegedly fraud against all defendants." (*Sic.*)

Bluebook:

"The judgment were [sic] entered on December 27, 1999."

Cross-references: Cal. Style Manual § 4:15[F]. Bluebook, Rule 5.2, p. 44.

§ 10:29 Quoting source containing error—Substantive errors

In the California Style Manual, when the error is substantive, such as mistakenly referring to the Code of Civil Procedure instead of the Civil Code or transposing the numbers in a code section, insert the correct information in brackets within the quotation, or in parentheses, or in a footnote. The Bluebook does not specifically address this issue.

California Style Manual:

"Section 11635 et seq. of the Code of Civil Procedure sets forth the rules of contract interpretation." (The intended citation is to the Civil Code, not the Code of Civil Procedure.)

"Section 11365[1] of the Civil Code sets forth the rules of contract interpretation."

---

[1] The intended citation is to section 11635, not section 11365.

Cross-references: Cal. Style Manual § 4:15[D].

§ 10:30 Quoting source containing error—Errors of omission

In both manuals, errors of omission are indicated by inserting the missing letter or word in brackets.

California Style Manual and Bluebook:

"The judgment [was] entered on December 27, 1999."

"The fourth cause [of] action alleges fraud against all defendants."

Cross-references: Cal. Style Manual § 4:15[F]. Bluebook, Rule 5.2, p. 44.

§ 10:31 Adding explanatory insertions to quoted material

In both manuals, when quoting a sentence taken out of context, it is sometimes necessary to insert a word or short clause in brackets to ensure that the intended meaning is clear.

"The minute order in the court's file stated that good cause did not exist to grant plaintiff's ex parte application [for an order shortening time]."

"The evidence proffered [the tape recording from defendant's answering machine] was not admissible since defense counsel failed to establish the necessary foundational basis for its introduction."

Cross-references: Cal. Style Manual § 4:15[F]. Bluebook, Rule 5.2, p. 44.

§ 10:32 Completing citations within quoted material

In the California Style Manual, when quoting a sentence that contains a reference to the name of a case or decision but either no citation or an incomplete citation, complete the citation by adding the missing information in brackets. Where no cite has been provided, provide the full citation in brackets.

In the Bluebook, no specific reference is made to this scenario, however, the following example is consistent with Bluebook format.

California Style Manual:

"She attempted to distinguish her case from *Buchan* [v. U.S. Cycling Federation (1991) 227 Cal.App.3d 134 [227 Cal.Rptr. 887]] by claiming that *Buchan* involved 'death defying' activities and presumably should not set the standard for determining whether lower-risk recreational activities involve a public interest."

Bluebook:

"She attempted to distinguish her case from *Buchan* [v. U.S. Cycling Federation, 227 Cal. App. 3d 134, 227 Cal. Rptr. 887 (1991)] by claiming that *Buchan* involved 'death defying' activities and presumably should not set the standard for determining whether lower-risk recreational activities involve a public interest."

The citation in brackets does not relieve the author of citing the case again in full the first time it appears outside the quoted passage.

Cross-references: Cal. Style Manual § 4:17.

§ 10:33 Adjusting quoted sentence for author's sentence

In both manuals, a quotation may only be grammatically correct (or make sense in the context of the sentence), if a singular noun or verb is changed to plural, or if the first letter of a word in the quote is changed from a capital letter to a lowercase letter. Such changes are acceptable provided the letter added, or the letter that was lowercased, appears in brackets.

California Style Manual and Bluebook:

The court rejected the argument, stating, "[N]ot every possible specific act of negligence of the defendant must be spelled out in the agreement."

In the instant case, both of these releases are similar to those examined in *Madison,* which were ultimately deemed "clear, unambiguous release[s] of all liability for any act[s] of negligence."

Cross-references: Cal. Style Manual § 4:18. Bluebook, Rule 5.2, p. 44.

§ 10:34 Line spacing and margins; multiparagraph quotes and block quotes

According to rule 201(c) of the California Rules of Court, quotations may be single spaced in pleadings. In papers submitted to the California Supreme Court, Supreme Court Rule 15(d)(4) requires that quotations over two lines in length must be block-indented by indenting from both the right and left margins.

In the California Style Manual, quotes may be indented from both the right and left margins, which is called "block-indenting." This style is most often used by practitioners since it clearly separates the quote from the body of the text. Paragraphs within quotations are indented just as they are in the original. While the quotation is single-spaced, double-spacing is used between paragraphs. No quotation marks are used when block-indenting the quotes. Quote citations are placed flush with the left-hand margin in the next line following the quote.

In the Bluebook, quotations of 50 words or more are single-spaced and block-indented. As in the California Style Manual, quote citations are placed flush with the left-hand margin in the next line following the quote. Quotations that are 49 words or fewer in length are enclosed in quotation marks and not block-indented.

Cross-references: Cal. Style Manual § 4:21. Bluebook, Rule 5.1, pp. 43–44.

§ 10:35 Quotations within quoted material

In both manuals, single quotation marks are used to indicate quotations within the quote.

Original:

An inanimate corporate entity that is run by directors "who are themselves
    defendants in the derivative litigation" cannot effectively waive a
    conflict of interest as might an individual under applicable professional
    rules.

Quotation:

The court unequivocally stated that "[a]n inanimate corporate entity that is
    run by directors 'who are themselves defendants in the derivative
    litigation' cannot effectively waive a conflict of interest as might an
    individual under applicable professional rules."

Cross-references: Cal. Style Manual § 4:22. Bluebook, Rule 5.1(a),
pp. 43–44.

§ 10:36 Quotation marks with other punctuation

In the California Style Manual, punctuation that separates the end of
the quote from the rest of the sentence (whether added by the author or
contained in the original quote) is enclosed in the quotation marks. Otherwise, punctuation is identical between the original and the quotation.

The judge stated he "was appalled" at such "outrageous tactics."

"What did you observe as you drove into the driveway?" the witness was
    asked.

Was the witness asked, "What did you observe as you drove into the
    driveway?"

Was it the plaintiff who said, "I'm sorry"?

The bailiff announced, "All rise!"

In the Bluebook, no specific reference is made to punctuation within
quotes, however, from the examples used therein, it appears that the format
is identical to the California Style Manual.

Cross-references: Cal. Style Manual § 4:23. Bluebook, see Rules
5.1–5.3, pp. 43–46.

§ 10:37 Footnotes in quoted material—Quoting footnotes in original

In the California Style Manual, when including an original footnote
from a quote, the footnote is given a new number in sequence with those
appearing in the author's text, and placed in brackets. The corresponding

footnote appearing at the bottom of the page is not bracketed. Immediately following this footnote number is the text from the original footnote in quotes. Alternatively, the original footnote text may be paraphrased.

The Bluebook does not address the format for quoting footnotes.

The following example shows the footnote number in brackets within the quote, and the two possible methods for setting forth the quoted footnote:

> In this case, the defendant was entitled to "*Cumis* counsel" since the "insurer [has] reserved the right to deny coverage at a later date." [3] (*San Diego Federal Credit Union v. Cumis Ins. Society, Inc.* (1997) 162 Cal.App.3d 358, 365.)

---

[3] "*San Diego Federal Credit Union v. Cumis Ins. Society, Inc.* (1997) 162 Cal.App.3d 358, 365, requires an insurer to pay for retained independent counsel for the defense of a lawsuit against the insured under circumstances in which the insurer reserves the right to deny coverage at a later date when punitive damages are at issue and the insurer denies coverage for punitive damages."

[*or*]

[3] In a footnote at this point, the author explained the role of "*Cumis* counsel."

Cross-references: Cal. Style Manual § 4:25[A].

§ 10:38 Footnotes in quoted material—Footnotes added to original

In the California Style Manual, when adding a footnote to a quotation, the footnote number is placed in brackets within the text. The corresponding footnote number appearing at the bottom of the page is not enclosed in brackets and is thereafter treated as any other footnote. The following example illustrates a quote to which a footnote has been added, in sequence with another footnote:

> The record states that "Defendant failed to appear at the Case Management Conference."[3] Thereafter, "an order to show cause hearing was held,"[4] and "sanctions in the amount of $150.00" were imposed against defendant.

---

[3] The conference was held on August 13, 1999.
[4] The hearing was held on September 28, 1999.

Cross-references: Cal. Style Manual § 4:25[B].

§ 10:39 Italics and underscoring in quoted material—Emphasis in original

In both manuals, language underscored or placed in italics in the original appears exactly the same way in the quotation. The phrase "original italics" or "original underscore" is not necessary since it is understood that the emphasis appears in the original.

However, when the original italics or underscoring are not necessary, they may be omitted provided the parenthetical note "(italics omitted)" or "(italics and underscoring omitted)" is inserted at the end of the quote.

Cross-references: Cal. Style Manual § 4:27[A]. Bluebook, see Rule 5.2, pp. 44–45.

§ 10:40 Italics and underscoring in quoted material—Emphasis added to quoted material

In both manuals, emphasis added to the quoted material to stress a point must be identified by the parenthetical phrase "emphasis supplied" or "italics added" following the quote.

California Style Manual:

Section 2033(b) provides that: "A defendant may make requests for admission by a party without leave of court *at any time*." (Italics added.)

"A defendant may make requests for admission by a party without leave of court *at any time*." (Code Civ. Proc., § 2033(b) (Italics added).)

Cross-references: Cal. Style Manual § 4:27[B]. Bluebook, Rule 5.2, pp. 44–45.

C. NUMBERS AND ITALICS

§ 10:41 General rules governing numbers

In both manuals, numbers that start sentences are spelled out. Numerals are used for dates, percentages (but "percent" is always spelled out except when used in tables), dollar amounts, decimal amounts, and time.

In the California Style Manual, the following general rules apply:

- Numbers zero through nine are spelled out.
- Numerals are used for numbers 10 and greater unless starting a sentence.

- Numerals are also used for units of measurement, time, or money.

- Commas separate numbers that follow one another.

- When an item is described by two numbers, the first number is spelled out (e.g., there were seven 6-foot basketball players; fifty $20 bills).

In the Bluebook, the following general rules apply:

- Numbers zero through ninety-nine are spelled out when used in text.

- Numbers zero through nine are spelled out when used in footnotes.

- Numerals are used for all larger numbers.

- Numerals are also used for dollar amounts, however, round numbers such as "million," "thousand," etc. may be spelled out.

- Commas are used to separate groups of three digits in numbers containing five or more digits (e.g., 1,234,567).

Cross-references: Cal. Style Manual § 4:28. Bluebook, Rule 6.2(a), p. 49. For specific rules for dates, time, numbers indicating sequence, percentages, fractions, ordinals, and money, see Cal. Style Manual §§ 4:25–4:33.

§ 10:42 Latin and foreign language words and phrases

In both manuals, Latin and foreign language words and phrases in common use are not italicized. The California Style Manual provides a list of Latin and other foreign terms that are not italicized (see Cal. Style Manual § 4:36[B]). It also provides a list of terms that are italicized (see Cal. Style Manual § 4:36[C]).

In the Bluebook, there is no comprehensive list of such words and phrases. However, there is a "strong presumption that Latin words and phrases commonly used in legal writing have been incorporated into common usage and should not be italicized."

Cross-references: Cal. Style Manual §§ 4:36[A]–[C]. Bluebook, p. 50, Rule 7.

D. PUNCTUATION

§ 10:43 Hyphens

The California Style Manual provides general guidelines for the use of hyphens, as well as lists of hyphenated and nonhyphenated terms. (For a list of hyphenated terms, see Cal. Style Manual § 4:43[B]; for a list of nonhyphenated terms, see § 4:44[B].)

In the Bluebook, there is no reference to hyphenated words per se, giving rise to the inference that conventional rules of grammar apply.

Cross-references: Cal. Style Manual §§ 4:40–4:45.

§ 10:44 Commas, semicolons, and colons

In general, follow the conventions of grammar applicable to commas, semicolons, and colons and see California Style Manual §§ 4:46–4:55.

§ 10:45 Apostrophes

In general, follow the conventions of grammar applicable to using apostrophes and see California Style Manual §§ 4:60–4:63.

CHAPTER 10
—Notes—

CHAPTER 10
—Notes—

INDEX